THE DISTINCTIVE WEDDING CEREMONY

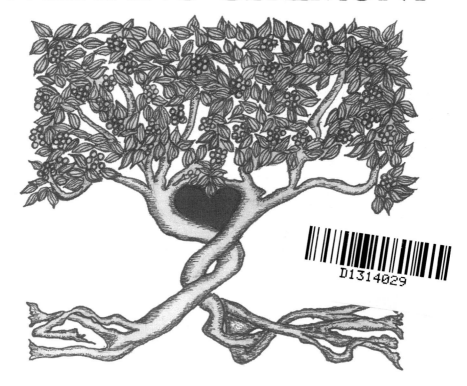

Planning Guide for Creating a Personalized, Unique
Ceremony, Supporting All Couples, Same Sex and Opposite Sex
or
How to Write your Own Vows
Ideal for Ministers and Online Officiants

REV. MARY CALHOUN

ISBN: 1493636421
ISBN 13: 9781493636426

TABLE OF CONTENTS

IN APPRECIATION

This book is dedicated to my clients. It has been shaped by your enthusiasm, insights, and values. Your faith in one another is a constant source of inspiration to me. Your trust in me acts as my daily ballast.

Thanks to Rev. June Robison, a pioneer minister who encouraged me to become a braver version of myself. To Janell, Leslie and Harry, for your honesty and countless hours of editing. To my sisters Julie and Fran, your encouragement and love help keep me strong. To my daughters, Jamela and Hillary, who are a continual source of love and laughter. To Kathy and Joey, for always nudging me forward. Thanks to my talented colleagues that have supported me through the years and continue to cheer me on — I am beholden. Because of you, my life is filled with miracles.

INTRODUCTION FOR ENGAGED COUPLES...

This comprehensive resource was written so that you are able to begin your wedding ceremony design process with ease and confidence. You are not only creating your ceremony, you are establishing a blueprint for your marriage as well. These words are important because they will become your personal covenant with one another.

Your ceremony is a personal amalgam of your Spiritual beliefs/shared values, peppered with natural emotional content, wrapped in a blanket of ritual and etiquette. (I define etiquette, as simply acting with grace and consideration to others while honoring your personal preferences.)

Weddings are frequently a reunion for both family and friends. It may be an opportunity for two families to bond for the first time. Weddings can also be a chance to heal old wounds. Whatever the case, it is the celebration of YOUR unique relationship and a rare occasion when *pure joy* is shared!

As a couple, take a moment to compose your *combined* vision for your wedding day. Be descriptive with adjectives: warm, genuine, intimate, fun, memorable. This vision will become your compass.

Choose your Officiant wisely. It is their responsibility to foster organization, decorum, humor, and soulfulness. They will set the temperature for intimacy and warmth. Your Officiant will connect the guests to *your* chosen words. Hopefully they will take some time to get to know you and this will be reflected in your personalized service.

From this book, you will choose one selection from each ceremony chapter. Some couples pick two choices from the Readings or Blessings. Frequently, the Wedding Couple *does not* select a Ritual or prefers to forego a Reading.

I strongly suggest that your final ceremony choices are kept private. This service is a gift to your loved ones and should be kept as *fresh as possible* for your wedding day. That said, it is likely that you will practice the Ring Exchange aloud during the rehearsal.

You don't have to memorize anything! When there is a "Repeat After Me," the idea is that your Officiant will feed you the words in small phrases. I have also included the "I Do" version of the Vows, so this will be comfortable for the more shy personalities.

Here is a pleasant flow of order for the wedding ceremony. This can be changed and adapted according to your preference.

- ❖ Invocations (Opening Statement)
- ❖ Blessing of the Couple
- ❖ Family Acknowledgements (Optional)
- ❖ Readings and Rituals (Optional)
- ❖ Exchange of Vows
- ❖ Exchange of Rings
- ❖ Final Blessings/Benedictions

Feel free to mix and match, taking an introduction from one selection and combining it with another choice. You will self-design so that this ceremony ends up reflecting you both as individuals and as a couple. It is an "a la carte" process.

You will need to choose the names that will be used throughout your ceremony. Example: Jennifer instead of Jen. Occasionally, individuals want to use the more formal version of their name during the service and then the casual version is used when speaking directly to one another during the Vow and Ring Exchanges.

Please keep in mind that an ideal ceremony is neither too long nor too short. Your guests should leave with a bit of inspiration. Efficient inspiration! Try for 20-25 minutes in length.

One of the greatest challenges for the Wedding Couple is to stay focused on the "why" of the event. The romance of the Wedding Couple can easily be lost in the myriad of details and the inevitable wave of stress that unfolds as they attempt to create their *perfect* wedding day.

I will strongly encourage you to tell each other *every day* why you want to marry the other. This little tradition will help keep you "crazy in love" during the time leading to your big day. And isn't this what your nuptials are all about?

My book is a culmination of the work that I have done with Wedding Couples (both straight and gay), over the past 20 plus years. I have created *The Distinctive Wedding Ceremony* with love and hope that it is instrumental in planning *your* day, a celebration that is a genuine reflection of both of *you*, your one-of-a-kind history and your hopes for the future.

Enjoy your journey,
Reverend Mary

MY FAVORITE WEDDING *MYTHS...*

Our "Best People" know what we expect of them...

When you invite your family members and friends to be an attendant in your wedding, be transparent about *YOUR* specific needs. Estimate the participation costs that members of your wedding party will incur. Pencil out the budget for the dress, shoes, tux rental, and plane ticket for the destination bachelor/bachelorette party. Give them fair warning of the estimated financial investment of being a key player. If you would like one or more of your attendants at a fitting, cake tasting or planning session, let her/him know up front. If your Best Person has an intense career path or is taking care of a baby, you may want to rethink your choice or lower your expectations. Let's say your attendant lives in another city and you need assistance building a custom arbor — you might consider finding a person more suited geographically to the tasks on your list.

We don't need an Event Planner...

Baloney. If you cannot afford a Professional Event Planner to help with the miles of details ahead of you, it is a stellar idea to ask a good friend, who excels at organizational skills, to help as your "Day Of" Coordinator. Having this person in place will help you *both* enjoy the day and be more relaxed. You can establish a wedding day timeline and submit phone numbers of vendors so your coordinator will call if someone is late. A "Day Of" Coordinator is essential to making things look seamless. You will never regret having someone in place to orchestrate your event. *See "Sample Timeline for the Wedding Day" on page 88 and "Sample Vendor List for the Wedding Day" on page 90.*

Let's *NOT* see each other before the wedding...

This tradition harkens back to the time of arranged marriages. Apparently couples were introduced to one another prior to the ceremony - and the outcome was not favorable! So the "unlucky to see each other before the wedding" superstition was born.

The day of your wedding will most likely be quite scheduled. This newer custom of couples seeing one another before the ceremony fosters intimacy and seems to have a calming effect on the Wedding Couple. If your photographer encourages you to have all those photos taken before the ceremony - he/she is brilliant! Seeing each other before the ceremony will make for a more magical wedding day – there is a reason this has become so popular. The "first look" is a *new* charming tradition. It is romantic and intimate. Indulge!

Programs are required...

These are done usually at the last minute. Programs take a good deal of time and seem to make Wedding Couples a bit crazy. And you get the added bonus of considering yourself "green"!!

Aisle runners...

This confuses Rev. Mary...the whole aisle runner thing. Aisle runners are often made of thin, flimsy, bonded paper. Because aisle runners are difficult to secure, they become wrinkled and torn. Even the "real carpet" runners buckle. They invariably trip members of the wedding party. On the day of the wedding, guests are NOT looking at the floor or the ground. They are looking at faces. If you have not purchased this hazardous item, save yourself some money. If you HAVE purchased one, return it, quickly. Aisle runners are a waste of money.

Let's put tall glass hurricane lanterns and vases in the main aisle...

My new personal favorite – glass in the main aisle at a wedding. Guests don't see them, knock them over and inevitably break the glass. Sometimes they contain candles. Recently a bride snagged a beautiful glass lantern (yes, containing lit candles) and was dragging it on her train down the aisle! Other mistakes: Trees in the aisle that restrict two people walking side-by-side. And the over-embellished Jewish Chuppah, (square trellis) where three people cannot comfortably stand upright.

Meet my cousin, The "DJ"…

Often the biggest mistake made is playing music via an iPod operated by a relative or wait staff. It is worth *every* penny to hire an *experienced* DJ. If you have more than 50 persons attending or if there is ambient noise at your venue, a microphone system must be set up. Your Officiant will need a wireless lapel microphone and your readers will need a hand held microphone – most likely on a stand. Frequently, Wedding Couples decide to write Personal Writings or Vows to one another. A hand held microphone is used for this as well. If your DJ or sound person suggests a stand microphone for your Officiant, patiently explain that it doesn't work well because they are handling their binder, jewelry, working with a Unity Candle, etc. for the ceremony.

Weddings are not complete without flower girls and ring bearers…

There is a trend to invite toddlers and wee people to join the cast of the wedding party. It makes for some rather challenging moments and upsets at the actual ceremony. Please don't feel obligated to have little ones in your parade. If the little ones you are considering are still taking naps, consider again!

Ushers must be enlisted…

And don't feel as if you need to select friends or relatives as ushers unless you have ample friends that need a purpose on the day of your wedding. Best Persons can double quite nicely. If you are determined to assign the title of "Usher" make certain that these people are assertive, friendly and willing to provide direction to your guests. Herding 150 people to their seats is not for the timid!

INVOCATIONS

On Being One Another's Compass

It is such a joy to be together today to celebrate the marriage of _____ and _____. We, their family and friends, recognize the divine path that brought them to this moment and are delighted to take part in this joyful day.

_____ and _____ have come to realize the importance that the other has played in balancing their life. That "going forward" would be incomplete without their cherished partner, their trusted confidante.

_____ and _____ recognize that in a healthy marriage, we become a compass for one another. Ultimately, we help the other person define who they are, who they will become and inspire them as they soar in their achievements. We encourage one another to evaluate intentions and priorities. We promote defined thinking and help to strengthen ideals. We enable our loved ones to celebrate what comes into our life and minimize what is lost.

As a guiding compass, we keep everything moving towards the direction of the sunshine. Towards possibilities.

_____ and _____ come together today, committed to this process of balance and guidance.

SIMPLE CONTENTMENT

_____ and _____ foster the conviction that life is best lived by weaving the principles of peace and tranquility into each day. They intentionally cultivate the values of ease and comfort, knowing this will help their marriage flourish.

Pam Brown wrote:

"Serenity does not cancel hope or adventure, work or love. It flows through the landscape of our busy lives, quiet and strong. Clear and gentle. Refreshing all we do or dream."

To discover joy in the common, to nourish lightness in the everyday routine, is the conscious act of choosing that which brings us simple contentment and promotes harmony.

_____ and _____ have each found a collaborator who earnestly values the evenness and sincerity of a joined life. With this resolve to share a union that is dedicated to cultivating amiability, _____ and _____ form a marriage grounded in serenity.

MARRIAGE AND ADVENTURE

We are gathered today to witness the union of _____ and _____ as well as give thanks for the path that led them to this delightful occasion.

These two believe that there is lasting strength when they share courage, stretch limits and embrace challenge. _____ and _____ realize that as they make discoveries together, they are able to blink with new awareness at the beauty of the earth and the glories of the heavens.

And it is not only outwardly that _____ and _____ intend to venture. They are committed to discovering new truths and cultivating fresh understandings of one another, as time goes on. An enhanced marriage is truly something they will continue to create every day. It is a sojourn with endless opportunities for personal transformations at every level.

Marriage is a pilgrimage, a journey undertaken for spiritual and emotional purposes, rich in adventure. An integrated discovery in tandem.

ON FAITH AND FRIENDSHIP

Margaret Boyd once said, *"Those who have hope have everything."*

Operating from faith and hope allows us great strength and fortitude. This elevated state of consciousness allows us to accomplish miracles – significant changes that might go unnoticed or unseen.

To grow a friendship, based on trust takes great faith for both persons. It also takes the ability to be vulnerable because every time we decide to invest more of ourselves in any significant relationship, we take a chance that the other person will hold us in precious esteem. As each of us individuals share this risk, we lose a little of our ego, which means that we make room for an expanded heart.

Faith allows us to see everything lit with hope and sparkle with gentle friendliness. It instills certainty in possibility. It transforms doubt into trust. Qualms are converted with confidence into a well-defined process. To share conviction, is to accept and unite one's purpose.

With hope as a compass, all things are possible.

So, we gather today to celebrate this power of reliance, love and friendship. In taking this leap of faith _____ and _____ demonstrate a determined belief in the future and God's divine plan.

And this is what we celebrate today – the expanded heart and soul of these two people.

ON SHARING

What a wonderful day to celebrate the marriage of _____ and _____. It is the beginning of a new and joined life. A marriage forged to create an enriched existence, abundant in all that is good.

When _____ and _____ co-mingle their joy, it brings enthusiasm to life and blesses all of us fortunate enough to share in the bounty of their love.

They will share their life-purpose, goals and dreams, for these will keep them consistently moving forward.

_____ and _____ will share pardon, asked for and given, it is the essence of a strong relationship.

They will bestow praise and appreciation on one another, as these gifts have the power to renew and enliven.

_____ and _____ will honor one another with truth. Kindly shared, it is the cornerstone of advancement.

By daily sharing these principles, _____ and _____ commit to building a union of deep compassion.

ON KINDNESS

_____ and _____ are aware that kindness is an essential component to their marriage. They recognize that consideration in matrimony takes on many forms and attributes.

We have all experienced thoughtfulness in the form of altruism, that ability to anticipate and give lovingly when one might be in need.

At times kindness takes on the persona of honesty, mildly given and neutrally received, truth can guide us in becoming a better person.

Caring shows itself by way of compassion, that ability to recognize when someone is hurting and then rising to support them, as best as we are able.

_____ and _____ have great reverence surrounding the benefits of true charity towards one another. They believe that it enriches their relationship with uncompromised loyalty and becomes their steadfast ballast. _____ and _____ appreciate that true kindness will kindle intimacy and respect in their future life together.

BRIGHT PERSPECTIVE

_____ and _____, we gather today in high spirits to celebrate your marriage. Your love of life and laughter affirms the positive and sends a fresh ripple of conviction to all.

You show us that each day brings its own gifts and promises us that with love, there is a fulfilling tomorrow.

_____ and _____ choose to embrace the adage that through laughter, we are able to *not only* endure – but thrive! That by taking each moment and making the best of it, one can overcome adversity. And when we are willing to keep our judgment soft, beauty and happiness can be found in unexpected places.

With their on-going commitment to elevate this relationship with their lighthearted approach, _____ and _____ enrich the landscape of faith for all of us, as they begin their new passage in life together.

BEST FRIENDS

Today we celebrate the power and endurance of friendship — for that is the true foundation of _____ and _____'s marriage. This bond has blossomed and changed with time and challenge, as all devoted friendships do.

It has been said that each friend represents a world within us — and perhaps that world is not born until the moment we meet. The "world" that is born, when one meets a kindred spirit, is an alliance of trust that allows us to begin to see ourselves through the loving perception of a friend.

Being one another's best friend is a constant lesson in both communication and compassion. It is an on-going process of being both teacher and student to one another. Of remaining distinct, yet woven, of being independent, but not isolated.

_____ and _____, your marriage will be a sheltered haven in which you can endlessly discover in the reflection of each other.

Friendship is the ability to hold a deep regard for another's goals, friends, relations, play and work. It is the unique ability to support and uphold emotionally, physically, spiritually and mentally, another being's essence and all that they hold dear.

And this is what we celebrate today.

INSPIRED LOVE

As we gather today to celebrate this joyous occasion, it seems only appropriate to take a moment to acknowledge our appreciation of _____ and _____ for sharing this sacred ritual with all of us.

Marriage is a fusion of your most intimate self with one other person, whom you can trust and turn to in times of need and joy. This unity means living with your best friend, someone you can give love to and receive love from, in a constant declaration of devotion.

This celebration today, of the blossoming of the heart, is a true inspiration to us all. Like spring – it brings a renewal, a certain rebirth, a reawakening of our capacity to share the affinity that so flavors the nuptial today.

Therefore we give thanks for the sweet happiness of _____ and _____. Their enthusiasm is appreciated as we witness these vows of great expectations and dreams.

May _____ and _____ be blessed in faith, understanding the ability to share compassion as they are united in all of their adventures, holding dear the fact that they have great strength in their willingness to grow beyond all limiting obstacles. They possess sincere gratitude for their foundation of unconditional love.

_____ and _____ are keenly aware that marriage is the joining of two lives; the spiritual, physical and emotional union of two human beings who have separate families, histories and traditions.

ON TOGETHERNESS

On this joyful day, _____ and _____ stand before us confident in their desire to combine their lives, their families, and their future.

_____ and _____ share the firm resolution of compromise, as well as the conviction to continually renew their commitment. Together they have chosen to uphold one another's ambitions, transcending setbacks by demonstrating positive reassurance and heartening comfort.

_____ and _____ have learned the value of success shared. They realize that when one of them attains an achievement – they both have accomplished the aspiration. These two recognize that joys are doubled in marriage.

They are also comforted in the knowledge that their challenges will be divided. Hand in hand, _____ and _____ are promising to show one another strength when difficulties interrupt their calm from time to time.

Today, we rejoice in their personal credence for abiding in togetherness, as it revisits for all of us the ideal principles of love and marriage and true friendship.

WEDDING BLESSINGS

A BLESSING OF TRANQUILITY

Bless _____ and _____ with the wisdom to constantly make this marriage a vital priority.

Allow this love to bless the world with hope and courage. Let their devotion and gentleness towards one another touch something wordless in all of us.

Guide them to create the precious time to rekindle and renew. Help them to know the calm of intimacy and the peace fostered by an unruffled life.

May they be blessed with gracious charity towards one another, always standing behind this marriage.

May _____ and _____ know the joy of seeking parallel pursuits in all of their endeavors of work and play; home and family.

And we pray, that the loving tranquility that emanates from this sacred union, inspires all of those around them, now and for all time.

Amen

BLESSING OF GOODWILL

_____ and _____, be mindful of the simple and intentional goodwill that will make this love a forever treasure. Hold your dreams dearly; plan for things that are important to you and we will all applaud your realized rewards. As a community, there is an emotional exchange of joy and spiritual communion when the whole of your life has leaned together to actualize an ambition.

May you find strength in serving one another in all the ways of the heart. You have been drawn to each other because you possess the attributes that will both encourage and challenge. May you each develop the very dimensions the other may lack, bringing balance and nurturing to your marriage.

May this process of personal transformation be gentle and may the resistance to change be swift. For this union is a partnership in which you both have roles of teacher and student.

As time goes on, you will continue to expand your characters and souls. May you each take pleasure in creating this life of compassion and may it be filled with ease and purpose.

BLESSING OF APPRECIATION

_____ and _____, it is our hope and prayer that you will be endowed daily with the graceful gift of gratitude.

To possess the gift of appreciation is to be wealthy in all-important ways. This richness of thanksgiving is perhaps the essence of renewal in all of our relationships.

The very act of acknowledging the good in our life allows our hearts to expand. It models gratitude to others. By mirroring kind affirmations to one another we validate the *holy*, the positive in our journey. And appreciation is certainly contagious!

_____ and _____, your loving gratitude will nurture patience, kindness and gentle caring.

Bless _____ and _____ with a marriage continually steeped in the rejuvenation of thankfulness. With this ultimate gift of charity they will foster respect and worthiness.

For as we bless, so are we blessed.

Amen.

BLESSING OF MUTUAL SUPPORT

Sharing is really the act of both giving and receiving. That flow that occurs between two people involving benevolence and a graceful ability to receive in return.

_____ and _____ know that love is without meaning if it is not shared continually.

They both recognize earnestly, the importance of filling one another's life with tranquility, so their affinity remains constantly nourished.

_____ and _____ understand that the tenderness of their warm touch each day will transcend the world's lack of gentleness. They know this ability to soothe is the balm of abiding comfort.

It is their mutual support that will act as a beacon to keep them inspired. It is their own potion of sunshine, their recipe of bringing sweetness to life.

It is our hope that each day remains bright for _____ and _____, enriched with the blessings of their union.

Amen.

A BLESSING OF HARMONY

We join in gratitude today for bringing _____ and _____ together in this Divine Plan.

We pray now that _____ and _____'s journey continues to be beautified with joys and graced with certainty. We ask that their passages are easy and their concerns are few.

Allow their life to be steeped in friendship, graced with contentment and may they always find time to notice the small miracles of everyday life.

Give them the wisdom to seek quiet, to speak gently to one another and act in constant charity.

May their sacred bond be forever held in harmony.

Amen

BLESSING OF RADIANCE

_____ and _____, it is our sincere and unified hope that God's light shines upon you and keeps you blessed in every possible way.

May you continue to rejoice in the *heaven* that you have found in one another, by continuing to embrace these essential elements:

May you know **Joy** – the internal radiance of leading your life from a loving demeanor

And **Truth** – the essence of which is consistency; the ability to act as you speak

Let **Faith** be your companion – encouraging acceptance through certainty and trust

Adopt **Gentleness** – the tender gift of peace and tranquility

And **Tolerance** – the skill of respecting opinions that are different, with understanding and compassion

Living by these convictions, _____ and _____ believe that they will continue to actualize a harmonious existence together. May they be delivered to grace each day.

Amen.

BLESSING OF FELICITY

We bless the numerous miracles that were intricately woven together that brought us to this moment.

It is our unified hope that _____ and _____ are filled with wisdom as they resolve the challenges that may find them. May they possess unbounded gratitude for their good fortunes and be able to continually enjoy life's daily treasures of joy.

We ask that they be dusted with courage and washed in unification as they continue on their way, helping them transcend every task into an opportunity.

Bestow upon them creativity in which to generate abundance in all ways.

Help them to validate the progress of small improvements. Let them feel the Rays of Lightness each day.

Grant them the music of laughter.

Allow them faith, hope and love.

Amen.

BLESSING OF FAITH

Marriage is an act of spiritual certainty. It requires great trust to pledge oneself for eternity - for all time. Today, _____ and _____ demonstrate their faith and belief in marriage, in life, in love.

We give thanks for this moment that brings _____ and _____ together in their commitment. We recognize the journey, the divine plan that brought them to this time. We pray that their joys be countless and their wounds be few.

Faith is forever kind, infinite in patience and wholly loving. Through faith the miracle of the relationship is refreshed and made new again.

Heavenly Father, give them the strength to keep the vows they make this day and cherish the love they share. May _____ and _____ support each other with faith, honesty, laughter and affection. Allow them to rejoice in their uniqueness, setting as their objective not to be identical, but to compliment each other. Let us, as their friends and family commit to support their goals and aspirations. For theirs is a divine mission.

Amen.

Blessing of Perfect Love

_____ and _____, may you be surrounded with this endowment of perfect and everlasting love for all time.

Allow it to rekindle your fellowship, inspire your challenges and motivate your adventures. Let your undivided love transcend the upsets and glorify the celebrations.

We, your community, join in common prayer, and ask that both your hearts remain earnest as you are realizing your dreams. We hope that you are always moving in the direction of possibility, while remaining grounded in your lifelong commitment of unconditional love.

May you serve as muse to one another, sharing understanding, humor, gratefulness and compassion. Honor one another with your understanding, challenge each other with gentle honesty and balance one another with creativity.

May you be blessed each and every day with these treasures — and may they multiply and echo with each passing year.

Amen.

SILENT RESPONSE PRAYER

The New Testament speaks to us about the power that is generated when two or more are gathered in prayer. So we'll honor that today with this unified blessing:

Heavenly Father, please guide us to encourage and hearten _____ and _____ in all their joys and disappointments. Allow us, as loving friends and family to commit to supporting their dreams and aspirations, standing beside them, not between them.

And we ask that they be richly rewarded in certainty, when doubt is present, laughter when judgment interrupts their mind's flow and unity above all else.

Give _____ and _____ the gift to travel light and journey lightly. Anoint them with ease through their trials and humble appreciation during their times of luxury. Help them to maintain their home as a peaceful sanctuary, offering warmth and safety to all.

May they perpetually give their faith to one another as our Father gives of Himself, gathering strength and wisdom in the years to come.

Bless _____ and _____ with renewal and comfort, knowing that perfect love is in all of us and from this comes compassion and understanding.

Amen.

FAMILY
ACKNOWLEDGMENTS

THANKSGIVING TO THE PARENTS

_____ and _____ would like to thank their parents for all they have contributed to their lives. They learned how to love because they were raised in loving homes.

They feel secure and confident in their relationship because, as parents, you allowed them to be independent. You've encouraged and supported them. You've taken pride in their achievements and nudged them toward their dreams.

You have modeled goodness, kindness, love, understanding, and nurturing. They trust that you will be there to celebrate their joyous times and support them during their struggles.

For these gifts they are both enriched and grateful.

IN GRATITUDE TO OUR PERSONAL COMMUNITY

_____ and _____ would like to take this opportunity – as love is being celebrated today, to recognize their family and friends.

They are grateful for the part that you have played in their lives. Through your gentle honesty and earnest support they have been able to better embrace their ideals. Because of your devotion, they have persevered through challenges as you lifted them upward and onward.

Your loyalty through the years has been a significant and essential element as they undertook new paths and fresh possibilities. Your friendship has been a compass helping them define a more passionate and joyful way.

For your contribution to their life, they are most thankful.

FAMILY PROMISE

(To be used when the couple has children.)

Note: The child(ren) of the couple is/are called forward at this time

Officiant: Do you _____ and _____ *(child's/children's name/s)* promise to help make this new family a positive union through your acceptance, love, cooperation, respect and forgiveness?

Child(ren): I do

Officiant: And do you _____ and _____, promise to assist your partner to parent this child/these children with encouragement, affection, patience, communication, love, laughter, playfulness and by modeling exceptional behavior: The most important being the ability to love one's self and the nurturing of your spouse.

Parents: We do.

Optional: Heavenly Father, bless this new family with Your strength and unconditional love. Guide them in their intentions to always be caring and loving. Show them how to be graceful in the presence of mistakes. Assist them to daily unfold as a unified and giving family during their process of overcoming setbacks and navigating new terrain. Hold their hearts and keep them close.

CALLING FORTH

The Wedding Couple occasionally chooses to use specific names in this passage.

When we join families in marriage, we share our history; we weave together our personal events and cultural traditions.

Family love is a shared awareness of time; a belonging to a treasury of stories that span generations. When we become a couple, we share this cognizance of time by sharing the memories and stories of our relations; our heritage.

It is based in their deep love of family that _____ and _____ would like to honor their beloved family members who have passed away and are unable to join us in a physical presence, but give their blessing on a spiritual level.

Let us honor these souls who are dearly cherished and remembered. Their influence on _____ and _____has helped guide their lives to this moment. Their work on earth has long been finished, but it is certainly not forgotten.

Let us share a united faith that these family circles are made complete, for this celebration today.

EXCHANGE OF VOWS

INTRODUCTION FOR VOWS

The Wedding Couple will be choosing ONE of these versions, either the "I Do" version or the "Repeat After Me" version. For the "I Do" version, the Officiant will ask each member of the Wedding Couple, individually, the questions, followed by the "I Do" response. For the "Repeat After Me Version," the Officiant will slowly and clearly say the phrases, in groups of three or four words, then pause for the repetition of the words, until the entire segment is recited by each member of the Wedding Couple.

When you are choosing one version over the other, please know that very few people are aware that *two* versions of this rite actually exist. First and foremost, be comfortable! If the "I Do" version seems easier and you will be more relaxed, be confident that your guests will not judge your choice. *If you wish to see helpful tips on writing your own Vows, refer to the "Writings and Readings Chapter" on page 65.*

VOWS OF SOLACE

Officiant:

These vows represent the very essence of your marriage, _____ and _____. Let the exchange of these promises serve to guide you always back to your place of solace, grace and understanding.

The "I Do" Version:

To the Wedding Couple:

Do you _____, take _____, as your husband/wife for today and for every day to follow? Do you promise to enlighten all of your days with calm in the midst of fear, patience in times of chaos, your caring service in times of sickness, and throughout it all, do you pledge to _____ the constant fidelity of your heart?

Response: I do.

The "Repeat After Me" Version

(Please note that these words are given to the Wedding Couple, individually, in groups of three or four words)

Wedding Couple:

I take you _____, as my wife/husband today and every day to follow. I promise to enlighten all of our days together with calm in the midst of fear, patience in times of chaos, my caring service in times of sickness, and throughout it all, I pledge to you the constant fidelity of my heart.

VOWS OF GRATITUDE

Officiant:

_____ and _____, may your marriage serve as a model to others of gratitude, devotion and a continual expansion of deep friendship. May God bless the conviction you make this day and may your sacred vows embrace you with the harmony and grace we celebrate at this moment.

The "I Do" Version:

To the Wedding Couple:

Do you _____, accept _____, as your finest friend and most intimate partner grateful for all that she/he brings to your relationship? Do you promise to stand beside her/him throughout the triumphant times as well as the days that will be filled with struggles, being true to her/him in all the ways of the heart?

Response: I do.

The "Repeat After Me" Version:

(Please note that these words are given to the Wedding Couple, individually, in groups of three or four words)

Wedding Couple:

I _____ accept you _____ as my finest friend and most intimate partner, grateful for all that you bring to our relationship. I promise to stand beside you throughout the triumphant times as well as the days that will be filled with struggles, being true to you in all the ways of the heart.

Vows of Sanctuary

"I Do" Version:

To the Wedding Couple:
Will you be _____ 's sanctuary? In your marriage, will you give and receive, discover and share, teach and learn? Do you promise to enjoy her/him when she/he is happy and comfort her/him when she/he is hurting? As her/his husband/wife, will you support, encourage and care for her/him, through all that life may bring?

Do you vow your unconditional support and exclusive devotion for all your days to come?

Response: I do.

The "Repeat After Me" Version:

(Please note that these words are given to the Wedding Couple, individually, in groups of three or four words)

Wedding Couple:
I will be your sanctuary. In our marriage we will give and receive, discover and share, teach and learn. I promise to enjoy you when you are happy and to comfort you when you are hurting. As your husband/wife, I will support, encourage and care for you, through all that life may bring.

I vow my unconditional love and my exclusive devotion for all our days to come.

VOWS OF MUTUAL RESPECT

The "I Do" Version:

To the Wedding Couple:
Do you _____ promise _____ your loving support and unfailing respect from this day forward? Will you be his/her ally in both the opportunities and challenges that the future will bring, secure in the knowledge that you will face your days together with mutual admiration? As his/her devoted wife/husband, will you always be faithful solely to him/her?

Response: I do.

The "Repeat After Me" Version:

(Please note that these words are given to the Wedding Couple, individually, in groups of three or four words)

Wedding Couple:
I _____ promise you, _____, my loving support and unfailing respect, from this day forward. I will be your ally in both the opportunities and challenges that the future will bring, secure in the knowledge that we will face our days together with mutual admiration. As your devoted wife/husband, I will always be faithful solely to you.

Vows of Partnership and Support

Officiant:

_____ and _____, you enter into this marriage as equal partners and share a keen understanding of the process of change and adaptation in relation to the health and well being of your marriage.

The "I Do" Version:

To the Wedding Couple:

Do you _____, promise to love _____ and live with her/him throughout this lifetime, building a caring and unified marriage? Do you vow to stand beside her/him through all of your adversities and triumphs, giving her/him unyielding support and above all, freedom to be herself/himself? Do you take _____, as your wife/husband and pledge to her/him your exclusive devotion?

Response: I do.

The "Repeat After Me" Version:

(Please note that these words are given to the Wedding Couple, individually, in groups of three or four words)

Wedding Couple:

I promise to love you _____ and live with you throughout this lifetime building a caring and unified marriage. I vow to stand beside you through all of your adversities and triumphs, giving you unyielding support and above all, freedom to be yourself. I take you _____ as my wife/husband and I pledge to you my exclusive devotion.

VOWS OF THE DIVINE

Officiant:

This "coming together" of _____ and _____, is the unification that happens through the traditional ritual of reciting of the Nuptial Vows. But it is not just the recitation of the vows that creates the Divine bond of marriage – it is the witnessing of these promises, as well, that gives credence and validity to this union today.

The "I Do" Version:

To The Wedding Couple:

Do you, _____, take _____, as your husband/wife, companion and partner for today and all of your tomorrows? Will you stand beside him/her to support and nurture him/her through all of his/her joys and sorrows? Do you promise your unfailing respect and loyalty.

Response: I do.

The "Repeat After Me" Version:

(Please note that these words are given to the Wedding Couple, individually, in groups of three or four words)

Wedding Couple:

I _____, take you, _____, as my husband/wife, companion and partner for today and all of my tomorrows. I will stand beside you to support and nurture you through all of your joys and sorrows. I promise my unfailing respect and loyalty.

Vows of Endearment

The "I Do" Version:

To the Wedding Couple:

Do you, _____, dedicate your life to _____, promising to share with her/him your gratitude, compassion and exclusive devotion? Will you encourage her/him through the challenges and joyfully celebrate the best of times, giving her/him all that you are and all that you will become?

Response: I do.

The "Repeat After Me" Version:

(Please note that these words are given to the Wedding Couple, individually, in groups of three or four words)

Wedding Couple:

I _____, dedicate my life to you, _____, promising to share with you my gratitude, compassion and exclusive devotion. I will encourage you through the challenges and joyfully celebrate the best of times, giving you all that I am and all that I will become.

Vows of Certainty

The "I Do" Version:

To the Wedding Couple:
Do you _____, take _____ as your faithful partner and one true love? Do you promise to lift him/her up during the challenges, lend him/her certainty when he/she is doubtful, and laugh throughout all of your adventures in life together? With your whole heart, through your whole life?

Response: I do.

The "Repeat After Me" Version:

(Please note that these words are given to the Wedding Couple, individually, in groups of three or four words)

Wedding Couple:
I take you _____, to be my faithful partner and one true love. I promise to lift you up during the challenges, lend you certainty when you are doubtful, and laugh throughout all of our adventures together. With my whole heart, for my whole life.

Vows of Affinity

The "I Do" Version:

To the Wedding Couple:
Do you, _____ take _____ as your wife/husband, and promise before God and these witnesses, to be a loving and faithful husband/wife; to be with her/him in times of comfort and in times of need, in both sickness and health? Will you offer her/him strength in her/his times of grief and sincere praise in her/his accomplishments? Do you commit to give her/him your deep respect and loving tenderness, as long as you both shall live?

Response: I do.

The "Repeat After Me" Version:

(Please note that these words are given to the Wedding Couple, individually, in groups of three or four words)

Wedding Couple:
I _____, take you _____ as my wife/husband and promise, before God and these witnesses, to be a loving and faithful husband/wife; to be with you in times of need, in both sickness and in health. I will offer you my strength in your times of grief and sincere praise in your times of accomplishment. I commit to give to you my deep respect and loving tenderness as long as we both shall live.

VOWS OF TRADITION

The "I Do" Version:

To the Wedding Couple:
Will you _____, have this man/woman _____ as your husband/wife, to live with you in a holy matrimony? Will you love him/her, comfort him/her, honor him/her and keep him/her in sickness and in health, in abundance and need, and forsaking all others, be faithful to him/her as long as you both shall live?

Response: I do.

The "Repeat After Me" Version:

(Please note that these words are given to the Wedding Couple, individually, in groups of three or four words)

Wedding Couple:
I, _____ take you _____, as my husband/wife. I promise to live with you in a holy state of matrimony. I will love you, comfort you, and honor you in sickness and in health, in abundance and need, and forsaking all others, be faithful to you as long as we both shall live.

EXCHANGE
OF RINGS

RINGS OF FRIENDSHIP

Officiant:

_____ and _____, these rings represent the covenant you have made to one another. May they serve to remind you both of your sacred union and the joy of today's celebration.

(Please note that these words are given to the Wedding Couple, individually, in groups of three or four words)

Wedding Couple:

_____, please accept this ring as a token of my love. May it serve as a constant reminder of our cherished friendship and these promises made this day.

RINGS OF LOVE

Officiant:

The Book of Corinthians tells us that there are three things that will last forever - faith, hope and love. It also says the greatest of these is love. _____ and _____ are exchanging these rings as symbols of the greatest, eternal gift to one another today... that most powerful love of which Corinthians refers.

(Please note that these words are given to the Wedding Couple, individually, in groups of three or four words)

Wedding Couple:

_____, just as this ring encircles your finger, going endlessly on, so will my love for, and commitment to you, continue for all time.

RINGS OF RADIANCE

Officiant:
May these rings always radiate with the joy and love we share today. Allow them to constantly dignify the vows that _____ and _____ hold dear.

(Please note that these words are given to the Wedding Couple, individually, in groups of three or four words)

Wedding Couple:
_____, I give to you this ring, as evidence of our exclusive bonds. In the future, may it always remind us of the *good* in our life.

RINGS OF ESSENCE

Officiant:
_____ and _____ have taken great care in choosing/creating these tangible emblems in the form of wedding rings, to signify their relationship, their history, and their future life together. May these rings be blessed with the essence of this day.

(Please note that these words are given to the Wedding Couple, individually, in groups of three or four words)

Wedding Couple:
_____, this ring is a token of my devotion and love. It is my intention that you wear it each day, knowing that I will continue to give to you, all that I am, all that I have.

Rings of Sincerity

Officiant:
Let these rings shine, through all of your days ahead, with the infinite joy and thanksgiving we share today. May they speak to you of your worthiness to be loved and to love – unbounded in all ways.

(Please note that these words are given to the Wedding Couple, individually, in groups of three or four words)

Wedding Couple:
I give you this ring, _____, thankful for the gifts you have brought into my life. Let it always surround your finger, reminding you daily of my sincere appreciation.

Ring Exchange of Infinite Reflection

Officiant:
_____ and _____, may these rings reflect your sacred and treasured alliance for all time. May they hold the memories of this day – unaltered – reminding you of the delight and grace that marked the exchange of these precious gifts.

(Please note that these words are given to the Wedding Couple, individually, in groups of three or four words)

Wedding Couple:
_____, please accept this ring, a loving sentiment of our journey, the past, the present and the future. May it embody our dreams, both actualized and those dreams yet to be.

RINGS OF DEVOTION

Officiant:

Let these rings be a visible sign that love is of the soul and represents your shared journey thus far, with the hopes and dreams of your future. Allow these rings to remind you frequently that love is a circle of contentment, delight and fulfillment.

(Please note that these words are given to the Wedding Couple, individually, in groups of three or four words)

Wedding Couple:

_____, with this ring I thee wed, for today and all of the years to come. May it serve as a symbol of my unending love and devotion. It will be constant reminder of our cherished friendship and these promises made this day.

RINGS OF UNITY

Officiant:

Let these rings, in their brilliance and strength, remind you both of your belief in your divine commitment. They are an outward visible sign of an inward spiritual unity.

(Please note that these words are given to the Wedding Couple, individually, in groups of three or four words)

Wedding Couple:

_____, I give you this ring, an age-old symbol of my devotion. May its presence on your finger be a constant reminder of our sincere covenant.

RINGS OF INSPIRATION

Officiant:

The circle is symbol of unending strength. May these keepsakes represent to _____ and _____ the brilliance of their future, inspired and bountiful in all ways.

(Please note that these words are given to the Wedding Couple, individually, in groups of three or four words)

Wedding Couple:

_____, let this ring inspire you to call to mind our love and the sweet contentment and devotion we share.

RINGS OF ACCORDANCE

Officiant:

May these rings serve to remind you both of the promises of this day and the gift of harmony that has so enriched your lives.

(Please note that these words are given to the Wedding Couple, individually, in groups of three or four words)

Wedding Couple:

Please accept this ring as a symbol of my appreciation for the love, laughter and understanding that you have brought to my life.

BENEDICTIONS

BENEDICTION FOR A GRACED LIFE TOGETHER

_____ and _____, may the Heavens hold your hearts close today and for every day to follow. May all of your desires and dreams shine with the brilliance of your loyalty to one another.

As you begin your life together, we pray that you are filled with a steadfast alliance to overcome all challenges. It is our hope too, that opportunities abound to continually enrich your journey and the fruits of your work bless you with purpose, contentment and abundance.

May your life together reflect the rewards of your companionship, always remembering the infinite possibilities born of faith.

Bless you, _____ and _____ in your nuptials today. Your love for one another is a seal upon your hearts from this day forward.

Pronouncement
Kiss
Introduction of the Couple

Final Blessing of Serenity

_____ and _____, may you be blessed with the kind of love that fosters serenity and compassion that reaches all, with courage that cannot be shaken and with faith strong enough for the challenges.

May God bless you with great prosperity, abundant joy and an ever-deepening bond, which is the Spiritual Nourishment for the souls of us all.

_____ and _____, may you preserve your ability to be a constant source of encouragement, humor, understanding and comfort to one another. It is our united hope that your life together is filled with innumerable days like this, filled with the same joy that encompasses us today.

Pronouncement
Kiss
Introduction of the Couple

Benediction of Tranquility

We are so grateful for your gift of sharing this inspired day with us, _____ and _____. We are united in our wishes for you:

❖ May you always be one another's best time and biggest comfort.

❖ May you both be able share laughter – especially during those times that seem to be lacking in illumination.

❖ That in each season, you are able to nurture your soul, as well as that of your partner.

❖ May your love and loyalty shine, so that others are inspired to risk *AND* love, as you have done.

❖ That you are able to see the miracles born of encouragement and change.

❖ May you continue to be grateful for the bounty in your life, your love, your family and your friends.

We are here to support you as a couple, to continue to share your tranquility, and soothe your hearts, in your journey ahead.

Pronouncement
Kiss
Introduction of the Couple

SENDING FORTH – GENTLE CARE

Each of us here today give _____ and _____ our love and best wishes.

May you both share a life of peace, playfulness and creativity. May you continue to know the pleasure of giving and the fulfillment of receiving. May you each be blessed with good health and encourage one another to take gentle care of your bodies, minds, and souls. May your honesty and forgiveness deepen your love each day.

Your love will inspire you when you are tired; it will soothe you when you worry; it will cleanse you when you are sick; it will keep you young, playful, and constantly embracing life. Your deep abiding comfort holds the power to transcend the world and all of its confusion.

May you be forever newly born in this love that we celebrate with you today.

Pronouncement
Kiss
Introduction of the Couple

WISHING YOU COMFORT

May your future be blessed with peace and tranquility, _____ and _____, holding for you a life of comfort, tenderness and joy.

We hope your days together are filled with supportive and inspirational friendships, nourished by your compassionate family and friends - and soothed by the gentleness of one another.

May you dwell in patience and tolerance; knowing that you are in the ideal place for your greatest enhancement.

We trust that hard work will be your ballast and amusing play will be your luxury.

And we wish too, that you are able to delight in the small everyday joys and sweet kindnesses that you will show to one another, for these are the elements of a contented marriage.

Pronouncement
Kiss
Introduction of the Couple

BENEDICTION OF JOY

As love is shared today, it is certainly multiplied. _____ & _____, we are so grateful for this opportunity to witness your vows and participate in the blessing of your marriage.

Going forth it is our unified hope that you are able to:

❖ Weave fun and laughter into the ordinary day

❖ Be each others best consoler

❖ Quiet yourself, so that you are able to hear the other

❖ Remember the charm of romance

❖ Value reciprocity

❖ Zealously pursue your aspirations

❖ And focus on the BEST in each other

And may today, your wedding day, be your happiest day "so far" and that it is followed by countless days to come - filled with unbounded joy!

Pronouncement
Kiss
Introduction of the Couple

BENEDICTION OF STRENGTH

_____ and _____, go into the world and fulfill your lives. Hold fast your ideals, keep sacred your shared and precious beliefs and the love of one another. Challenge one another that you may continue to flourish spiritually and accept the treasures of growing older together, providing strength where there is weakness. For you will find great power in serving one another in continual collaboration.

We hope that your days together will be rich in laughter, comfort, purpose, reflection and appreciation. For these are the ingredients for a life filled with joy, health, creativity, and wellbeing. This is a marriage abundant in strength, blessed with compassion, and radiant in love.

And this is what we wish for you today!

Pronouncement
Kiss
Introduction of the Couple

FINAL BLESSING OF HEARTH AND HOME

We are united in our best wishes for you _____ and _____. And it is our hope that you are blessed by the warmth and nurturing of your home – wherever it may be.

❖ Let it be a place filled with ease and happiness, creativity and learning.

❖ That you are able to create a haven radiant in warmth and that all of your friends and family may be welcomed by your good graces and hospitality.

❖ Let this sanctuary be infused with your ever-growing love and that you return to it each day to renew, rekindle, and be nourished.

_____ and _____, we wish you an enriched life in which you kindly take care of one another and that you are surrounded by your loving family and dear friends.

Pronouncement
Kiss
Introduction of the Couple

BENEDICTION OF THE INFINITE POWER OF LOVE

We have witnessed today, the commitment of your love to one another, _____ and _____. You have allowed us the privilege of seeing directly into the very essence of your marriage. We celebrate with great joy in your fulfillment today.

❖ May you be blessed with the ability to bathe one another's mistakes in a graceful light.

❖ May you give yourself completely to one another, each and every day.

❖ May you share faith when there is doubt.

❖ May life bestow upon you, wholeness of mind, body and Spirit.

❖ May you build each day on the foundation that you are able to gather strength from one another, knowing that you are better together than either of you are apart.

❖ May you always remember the essential power of infinite love.

Pronouncement
Kiss
Introduction of the Couple

FINAL BLESSING OF CELEBRATION

_____ and _____ love will be the key ingredient in joyful times and the strength that will see you through your darker moments. The miracle of love will be more powerful and encompassing than any of the changes life will offer you.

May your home be filled with laughter, music, creativity, knowledge and affection. May it be a place frequented by beloved family - and old and new friends, alike.

We ask God to bless you on your journey – the exacting challenge of creating a nurturing, stable and harmonious relationship in the face of your daily cycle of concerns. May your days of embracing your relationship, be gentle and soothing; both of you knowing the most difficult task may be to remain individuals all the while maintaining an essential intimacy.

We pray, that you can together, make opportunities out of challenges, being so keenly aware, that there is strength in numbers. May you be graced with the benevolence to ask for and give pardons generously. That compromise and intimacy frequent your conversations and your loving sense of fun and affection remain spontaneous.

We're here to celebrate with you today, to toast, to laugh and join together, beholden that true destiny has fulfilled itself – your happiness is certainly shared! Please remember that you are dearly loved and that we are united in our best wishes that all your many days together be filled with joy and magic.

Pronouncement
Kiss
Introduction of the Couple

RITUALS

Rituals are usually placed just before the Vows in the order of service. If you are having a Reading as well, the Reading(s) will come before the Ritual.

UNITY CANDLE (COMING HOME)

Optional:

_____ and _____ would like to call their mothers forward at this time for the Unity Candle Ceremony. This ceremony is a simple act representing the unification of two families and they honor their mothers at this time; dedicated women who have been their ardent supporters and biggest fans, always giving their unfailing guidance and love.

Ceremony:

To _____ and _____ this candle symbolizes the contentment and comfort that they find in one another, and the time they share. The harmony acknowledged at this moment is the "coming home" – that peace, sought and found, which we celebrate today.

UNITY CANDLE OF SINCERE INTENTION

_____ and _____ will now light the Unity Candle. For them, it represents the leaving behind of their single, independent lives for a journey of unification.

They realize that their unique blending of hopes and dreams is a precious wholeness. That this integration will be a solace and balm each and every day.

Let this light forever represent their sincere intention to uphold one another, making way for heartened happiness and fortified devotion.

May sweet Spirit bless all of their days with this sustained Unity.

Blessing of the Hands

(Author Unknown)

These are the hands of your best friend, young and strong and full of love for you, as you promise to love each other today, tomorrow, and forever.

They will be there working alongside yours, as together you build your future.

These are the hands that will passionately love you and cherish you through the years, and with the slightest touch, will comfort you like no other.

They will hold you when fear or grief fills your mind.

These are the hands that will tenderly hold your children (or pets/grandchildren).

Your hands will countless times wipe the tears from your eyes; tears of sorrow, and tears of joy.

As these hands share affection, you demonstrate your love for one another — the greatest foundation in holding your family as one.

And lastly, these are the hands that even when wrinkled with age, will still be reaching for yours, still giving you the same gentle tenderness with just a touch.

A FEW OTHER RITUALS

There are as many Rituals/Traditions as there are cultures. Many versions of Rituals may be found on the Internet.

Jewish:	The reading of the Seven Blessings; The Breaking of the Glass
Filipino:	The Veil and Cord Ritual
Buddhist:	The reading of a Metta
Hindu:	A reading from the Rigveda
Native American:	Blanket Ceremony
Asian:	Wedding Tea Ceremony (adapted)

The Sand Ceremony: Different colors of sand are poured into a common vase. *(Either Unity Candle Ritual in this chapter may be adapted.)*

Wine Ceremony: Two different colors of wine are poured into a common carafe. *(Either Unity Candle Ritual in this chapter may be adapted.)*

Handfasting: The Wedding Couple's hands are bound by a cord or ribbon. Mothers frequently tie this binding. *("Blessing of the Hands" in this chapter works well for this.)*

Flower Ceremony: Members of the family place different varieties and colors of flowers in a large bouquet, representing their diversity.

Ring-Warming: For a small gathering, the wedding rings are passed from the back to the front, with each guest taking a moment to silently give their wishes/blessings. The rings will finally be handed to close family members in the front row and then handed to the Officiant before the Wedding Couple exchanges them.

INGENUITY REPEATING ITSELF

Inspiration is often found close to home. My clients, Annie and Nicole, adopted this idea from Annie's mother and father. A statement was written on a "Witness Scroll" placed where guests could sign it during the reception, much like a guest book.

The wording on this declaration of support was taken directly from the scroll used by Annie's parents, Jack and Ruth, 37 years previously on their wedding day: *"We rejoice in the love that they share. We will strive to support them as they seek the varieties and realities of the deep and everlasting love they have pledged to each other on this day."*

Jack and Ruth's original scroll was framed and on display near Annie and Nicole's new scroll. The nostalgic display was made complete with a well-loved wedding photo of Ruth and Jack.

WRITINGS
AND
READINGS

If you are having a Reading, this usually takes place before the Vows. If a Ritual has been selected as well, a nice flow would be: Reading, Ritual, Vows. If you have written something you would like to read to one another and still include one of the Vows from this book, you might place it before the Vow Exchange.

COMPOSING YOUR OWN VOWS, LETTERS, OR PERSONAL WRITING

Many Wedding Couples wish to make their ceremony more personal by writing their own vows. Sometimes this creative endeavor takes the form of letters or writings to one another. Here are some helpful tips.

Write first and then decide if your words are creative writings, a story, a statement, a letter – or they just may be the actual VOWS!

Check your state guidelines to see if specific promises, words or phrases *must* be included to make the marriage legal. This varies from state to state.

Decide whether your respective writings are to be shared or kept secret from one another until the actual wedding day. If these writings will to be kept secret, perhaps you would feel comfortable sharing the word count with each other. Your creative script should be short and sweet in length. Two or three minutes would be a good duration of which to aim. Your Officiant might help you edit your work.

Vow Tip: Vows are specific about what you will do during the course of your marriage. You promise to nurse them while they are sick, remain monogamous, be supportive and loving ... for a lifetime!

Carry a journal with you for the next several weeks and write about the following:

❖ Document your personal history. How did you meet? What magical, divine work was at play?

❖ What favorite things do you have in common?

❖ How do you balance one another?

❖ List your favorite travels.

❖ Why do you want to marry him/her?

❖ What do you both find funny and makes you laugh?

❖ How do you feel when you are reunited after being apart?

From this collection of notes, you may discover the essence of your relationship. Now it is time to begin the editing process. As you hone and fine-tune these words, a theme will emerge. Stay with it. Try to avoid clichés and over-used words. *Remember that the spoken word is much different than the written word. Read your final versions aloud. Ask a trusted friend to give honest feedback.*

READINGS FOR YOUR WEDDING

The poems and writings listed below are proven favorites and readily accessible on the Internet. Most of us own a book filled with favorite poetry. If not, perhaps it is time to purchase one! Be creative and resourceful when choosing a reading. Make certain that it fits you both well.

Love
By Roy Croft

On Marriage
By Khalil Gibran

The Art of Marriage
By Wilfred Peterson

Blessings of the Apaches
Author Unknown

My Love
By Linda Lee Elrod

To Love is Not to Possess
By James Kavanaugh

Union
By Robert Fulghum

How Falling in Love is Like Owning a Dog
By Taylor Mali

First Corinthians (13: 4 — 8)
New Testament

As You Like It
By William Shakespeare

The Kama Sutra of Kindness
By Mary Mackey

When You Love Someone
By Anne Morrow Lindbergh

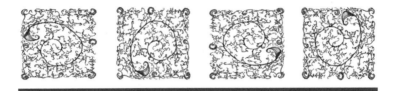

ORCHESTRATION

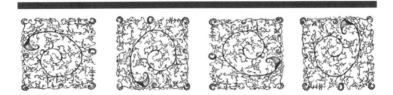

Formal Escorting, Processional and your VIP Ceremony Seating Chart

The Formal Escorting

The formal escorting happens after all the guests are seated and before the processional. The grandparents of the Wedding Couple are seated first, followed by the parents. In the past, ushers would typically escort this group. Since this meant that total strangers were walking down the aisle together, society now embraces a more personal style.

If grandparents, as a couple, are capable of walking independently, perhaps they will walk together. Their children or grandchildren are often paired as escorts. Grandparents are usually seated in the front two rows. *Please see the "VIP Ceremony Seating Sample" page 80.*

If your grandparent(s) will need special help being seated, (wheel chair or walkers) they may prefer to be pre-seated. Ask your grandparents about their preference. You will want everyone to feel comfortable. Consider asking a family member to stay with your grandparent(s) to chat after they are seated, so that they are not sitting alone before the wedding.

Once in a great while, The Wedding Couple has special aunties or uncles in the formal escorting. Godparents have also been given this honor from time to time.

It is common for the parent(s) of one or both member(s) of the Wedding Couple to escort their spouse to their assigned seat and then circle around to escort their child in the processional.

The topic of stepparents being included in this formal escorting may surface. This is a case-by-case basis. Ultimately, this must be your decision. Keep in mind, that it is an *earned honor* to be chosen to participate in the formal escorting. And yes, you may pre-seat stepparents.

The Processional

Please see "The Traditional Processional" on page 78 and "Paired Processional" diagrams on page 79.

Like the rest of your ceremony, this will be a personal series of decisions that the Wedding Couple will make together. This discussion is best done privately, without input from your families.

There are many options for how the wedding party will ultimately gather in the front Altar Area at the beginning of your ceremony.

Frequently the Wedding Couple wish to be escorted by their parent(s). But not always.

Creative Variations for the Formal Escorting/Processional:

❖ The Wedding Couple walks in together.

❖ Each member of the Wedding couple, escorted by their parents, one following the other, at the end of the Processional.

❖ When either member of the Wedding Couple has children, the children enter with their mother or father.

❖ Mother escorting the Bride.

❖ Bridesmaid (sister) escorting Father of Groom/Bride (she returns to enter with wedding party).

❖ Groomsman/Best Man (brother) escorting in Mother of Bride/Groom (returns to enter with wedding party or stands up front).

❖ In the case of *two* dedicated fathers or mothers, they BOTH might escort either member of the Wedding Couple.

❖ The Groom or Bride enters and stands up front. The other makes their grand entrance and begins their walk up the center aisle. The first party walks halfway down the aisle then they walk together to the front "Altar Area."

❖ Grooms are selecting female attendants and Brides are choosing their guy pals as to stand up with them.

❖ Groom enters with Officiant, either from the center aisle or from the side aisle.

Please do not concern yourself if you have different numbers of attendants standing on each side up front. You do not need the same number of Best People. Two male attendants may escort one female attendant. Alternatively, one groomsman might escort two bridesmaids. Groomsman can walk in together. Bridesmaids can be paired. Lots of options here!

Music

A simple strategy is to select just THREE songs. One piece will be for the formal escorting *and* processional. Any experienced DJ is able to "loop" the music and then fade it when the entire wedding party is in place – regardless of how many people are walking down the aisle. The second piece of music is usually for the grand entrance, when everyone stands up. The third piece of music will be reserved for the recessional/exit - following the Introduction of the Wedding Couple. If this is a very small wedding party with a brief walk, consider just two pieces of music: one for the entrance, one for the exit.

The music seems like a simple detail but it can be VERY tricky. Some Wedding Couples want to use iPods. Seldom do they consider the speakers or who is going to play the music. Invariably the music does not fade. It just abruptly ends in a very awkward fashion. *DO NOT UNDERESTIMATE THIS CRUCIAL PART OF YOUR CEREMONY.* The music person should arrive at least one hour prior to the wedding start time to set up and practice the music. And by no means should either member of the Wedding Couple try to be DJ for the day! You will also need about 45 minutes of background music to be played while guests gather, mingle and are seated waiting for the wedding to begin. Your DJ will have a library of easy listening music for this purpose. Your live musicians will be familiar with soothing arrangements.

Flower Girls and Ring Bearers

These young attendants are NOT required for your ceremony to be complete. It is a LOT of extra effort to have children involved at a wedding. Especially little ones under the age of five! I recently had a two-year old flower girl trip a bridesmaid.

Unless the children are over the age of nine years old, it is advised that they do not stand up front with the attendants during the ceremony. I suggest that they sit with the guests and have adult supervision. Their attention span is typically not developed for the 25 minutes it takes to stand up front. Please *do not* designate your parents as nannies for the ceremony. They deserve to enjoy this moment and be able to focus on YOU.

If these children are younger than five years of age, we place them before the wedding party's entrance in the processional. The little ones do not enter just before the grand entrance. In this way, if there is any disruptive behavior, decorum is regained before the grand entrance! *The real rings are not given to children. Fake rings will be tied to the pillows.*

Great Tip: When making your VIP Ceremony Seating Chart, space the children of the wedding party in between supervising adults. Prepare a quiet activity bag for them — a little surprise they will find on their designated chairs after their walk down the aisle. A small notebook and pencil will keep them busy during the service!

Pets in the Parade

More frequently it is becoming common for the Wedding Couple's beloved pet to be part of the ceremony. There may be strong rules regarding animals at the venue that you are renting. Be clear about the regulations and if you are granted permission, *get this promise clearly in writing.*

Large groups may overwhelm even the sweetest of dogs. It is a great idea to bring your canine friend to the rehearsal so you have some idea of their behavior in a new setting with a large group of people. Overwhelmed dogs have howled throughout the entire ceremony. Make certain that you have a *dog handler* present at the ceremony — just in case your pet becomes upset. You will want everyone to be able to focus on the actual wedding. Make plans for canine care during the reception. *As a final word of caution, do not place real wedding jewelry around the dog's neck!*

VIP Ceremony Seating Plan and Nametags

Please see "The VIP Ceremony Seating Sample" on page 80 and "The VIP Ceremony Seating Template" on page 81.

You will be making your own VIP Seating chart and creating ceremony nametags for the VIP chairs. This will save much confusion and gives your wedding party a clear plan as to who specifically has reserved seating. Note: this is *critical* with large or divorced families. Neither the ushers nor your relatives will know what your expectations are without this blueprint.

This VIP seating area traditionally has a designated "side" that represents each member of the Wedding Couple. Behind this, all the other guests will be seated without preference to the Wedding Couple's different sides. It is all mixed seating!

When you design your VIP Ceremony Seating plan, be sure to include readers, flower girls, ring bearers, their parents and the singer that might be participating in the service. Designated end aisle seats are best assigned to these ceremony participants. In this way, they are able to find their seats after they walk down the aisle or come to the front when it is time for them to read or sing.

The Event Coordinator at your venue will know how many chairs will fit across each row, depending on your specific room layout.

Once you have filled out "The VIP Ceremony Seating Template," you will create nametags that will be placed on, or taped to the chairs. Note: the tag is taped where one's back will be when a person sits in the chair. If you will be using cloth chairs or fabric covers, you might produce a "tent style" of card that is folded and placed on the seat of the chair. If you are outdoors flat cards may blow away with the slightest breeze. When you design your VIP seating chart and make your nametags: PRINT CLEARLY!

The tags can be produced quickly and easily. Cut small, 2" x 3" rectangles of heavy stock paper and print all the family names that will be seated in the first few rows of your ceremony on each card. Or you can use your home printer and paper cutter. Easy!

If you have a "Day Of" person, he/she can be in charge of tagging the chairs. Otherwise a trusted friend can be asked to arrive early and take care of this duty. If you are using tape - make certain that you include clear tape to go with your chart and tags for the person assigned to the chair tagging task.

Your VIP Ceremony Seating chart will need to be prepared by the week of your wedding so that it can be used during the rehearsal.

Traditional Processional

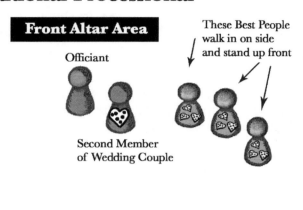

Front Altar Area

Officiant

Second Member
of Wedding Couple

These Best People
walk in on side
and stand up front

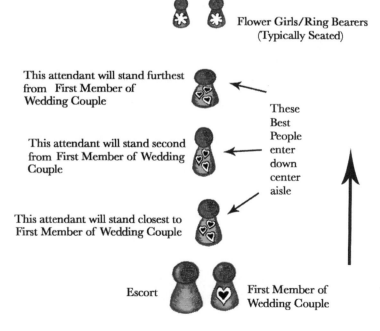

Flower Girls/Ring Bearers
(Typically Seated)

This attendant will stand furthest
from First Member of
Wedding Couple

This attendant will stand second
from First Member of Wedding
Couple

These
Best
People
enter
down
center
aisle

This attendant will stand closest to
First Member of Wedding Couple

Escort

First Member of
Wedding Couple

Paired Processional

Front Altar Area

Officiant

Second Member
of Wedding Couple

This attendant will stand furthest away from First Member of Wedding Couple

This attendant will stand furthest away from Second Member of Wedding Couple

This attendant will stand second from First Member of Wedding Couple

This attendant will stand second away from Second Member of Wedding Couple

This attendant will stand closest to First Member of Wedding Wedding Couple

This attendant will stand closest to Second Member of Wedding Couple

Escort

First Member of
Wedding Couple

VIP Ceremony Seating Sample

Front Altar Area

Officiant

First Member of Wedding Couple   Second Member of Wedding Couple

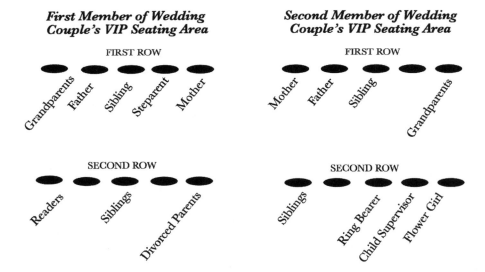

First Member of Wedding Couple's VIP Seating Area

FIRST ROW

Grandparents Father Sibling Stepparent Mother

SECOND ROW

Readers Siblings Divorced Parents

Second Member of Wedding Couple's VIP Seating Area

FIRST ROW

Mother Father Sibling Grandparents

SECOND ROW

Siblings Ring Bearer Child Supervisor Flower Girl

Note: If the parents are divorced and the situation is strained, place "cushion" people between the parents or seat a parent in the second row. For the guest rows that come after the VIP Ceremony Seating area, it is just "festival seating" because seldom are there equal number of guests. Added bonus: this promotes mingling. Your Event Coordinator at your venue site will enlighten you regarding the number of chairs that will be placed across each side of the aisle based on the ideal facility setup or your specific scheme. Readers are placed on the same side as the microphone setup.

The VIP Ceremony Seating Template

Front Altar Area

Second Member of Wedding Couple's VIP Area

First Row

Clearly print names here

Second Row

Clearly print names here

CENTER AISLE

First Member of Wedding Couple's VIP Area

First Row

Clearly print names here

Second Row

Clearly print names here

Contact the Event Coordinator at your venue regading the number of chairs that will be placed in each row.

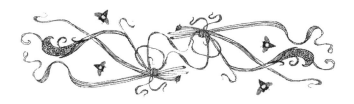

PRIOR DETAILS

WEDDING COUPLE'S PRE-WEDDING CEREMONY CHECKLIST

To be completed at least two weeks prior to the wedding day.

❖ Because the Officiant and/or "Day Of" Coordinator will be interacting with your family and friends, it would be a great asset for them to receive a short biographical list, (Bio List) of your nearest and dearest. This would include your parents, stepparents, siblings, grandparents, attendants, flower girls, ring bearers, and readers. This Bio List will foster a warmer connection at the rehearsal and on your wedding day. Each member of the Wedding Couple will compose their own list. This is an essential tool when trying to navigate the waters of a divorced family. Let your "Day Of" Coordinator and Officiant know that these Bio Lists are to be kept confidential. The added benefit to preparing this list: It serves well when creating your formal escorting plan and processional scheme, as well as the VIP Ceremony Seating chart!

Sample Bio List:

Mother of the Groom: Susan Channing Lives in Boulder, CO. Single, works for accounting firm, likes to rock climb. We are very close.

Father of the Groom: Charles Binder Resides in Alameda, CA. Married Carol in 1994. We make an annual trip to Napa and enjoy their company.

❖ The VIP Ceremony Seating chart indicates where the families of the Wedding Couple and the ceremony participants (readers, flower girls, ring bearers), will be seated. At least three copies are needed: one for the person in charge of tagging chairs, one for the Officiant, and the Wedding Couple will keep one copy as backup. *Please see "VIP Ceremony Seating Sample" on page 80 and the "VIP Ceremony Seating Template" on page 81.*

❖ Make certain that the Person Running the Rehearsal ("PRR") or Officiant understands the nuances of running a rehearsal. *Please see the "How to Organize and Conduct a Rehearsal" on page 106 in the "Rehearsal Scheme" Chapter.*

❖ Clearly print nametags for the VIP chairs. *Please see "The VIP Ceremony Seating Sample" on page 80.*

❖ Type your selections to the ceremony that you have chosen and email to the Officiant. If you have chosen Readings and/or Writings you will send them along as well.

❖ Select the Music. Choices are typed and submitted to DJ/Musicians/Designated Music Person/Musicians. Usually three songs are needed for the actual ceremony: one (4+ minute) song for formal escorting (it is often "looped" for the processional), and one for grand entrance and one for recessional/exit. If you are doing your own music, don't forget to select 45 minutes of background music to be played as guests gather and are being seated for the pre-ceremony period. If the wedding party is small and the walk is short, one song for the entrance and one song for the exit may be suitable.

❖ Purchase ritual items. You don't need to invest in the expensive Unity Candle Ceremony sets in stores or online. Go to your favorite craft supply store and buy, in your color of choice, one large pillar candle and holder (if doing this out of doors, you will need a hurricane lamp as well), two tapered candles and holders, two 2-inch votive holders and candle (taller than tea lights), and one butane lighter. Light the large pillar candle for about an hour sometime before your wedding day. This will allow it to light more easily at the actual ceremony. *Specific instructions for the Unity Candle Ceremony are found in the "Officiant's Pre-Wedding Overview" on page 99.*

❖ Purchase items for any children involved in the service (ring pillows, flower baskets, quiet activities to place at their seats).

❖ Send reading(s) to reader(s).

❖ Legal documents/marriage certificate obtained from local government agency. Each state, county or parish has specific laws and regulations: best to research this early. *Note: Some states require a waiting period after the license is issued.*

❖ Send diagrams for the Processional and the Formal Escorting to the Officiant. At least five sets of diagrams are needed for the wedding: one for Officiant, one for "Day Of" Coordinator, one for Event Coordinator at the venue, one for DJ/Musicians, and one for the Wedding Couple as backup. *Please see Processional diagrams on page 78 and 79.*

❖ Prepare the Introduction of the Wedding Couple after the Officiant pronounces them. If an introduction is made after the kiss, the Officiant will introduce the Wedding Couple as either "The Happy Couple" or "Chris and Pat Hudson" or the traditional "Mr. and Mrs. Chris Hudson." The Officiant needs to know the Wedding Couple's preference.

❖ Prepare copies of "Timelines for the Wedding Day" for all family members, attendants and ceremony participants. *Please see "Sample Timeline for the Wedding Day" on page 88.*

❖ Prepare three copies of the "Vendor List" one for the "Day Of" Coordinator, one for Event Coordinator at the venue, one is kept by the Wedding Couple as backup. *Please see "Sample Vendor List for the Wedding Day" on page 90.*

❖ If you do not have a professional Event Planner hired, collect/purchase items for your Emergency Kit. *Please see "Emergency Kit List" on page 92.*

❖ Inform your Officiant if you have made any changes in the wedding ceremony, Formal Escorting or Processional diagrams since you have last communicated with him/her. Surprises at the rehearsal will consume time and become confusing for key players.

CEREMONY VOCABULARY AND ACRONYMS:

Wedding Couple: Traditional term would have been "Bride and Groom"

MOB: Mother of Bride

FOB: Father of Bride

MOG: Mother of Groom

FOG: Father of Groom

SMOB: Stepmother of Bride

SFOB: Stepfather of Bride

SFOG: Stepfather of Groom

SMOG: Stepmother of Groom

MOH: Maid or Matron of Honor

BP: Best Person/People (one of the Attendants of either sex)

Attendant: Friend or relative, close to one or both of the members of the Wedding Couple

Wedding party: Attendants standing up front with Wedding Couple for ceremony

Ceremony participant: Reader, singer, flower girls, ring bearers

Altar Area:	Front of ceremony, where the wedding ceremony takes place
PRR:	Person Running Rehearsal
FG:	Flower girl
RB:	Ring bearer
Witnesses:	Persons signing the legal documents after the ceremony.

(Sample Timeline for the Wedding Day)

Timeline for Chris and Pat's Wedding Day – June 15th
"Day Of" Coordinator: Molly Smith: Mobile: 123.456.7890

Time	Involved Parties	Location/Activity
9:00 a.m.	Pat, Best Person Note: bring shoes + clothing	Pat's home Hair, Makeup
10:00 a.m.	Chris, Best Persons	Deliver wine to venue
	Photographer arrives Getting ready photos	Pat's house
11:30 a.m.	Chris, Best Persons	Venue, getting dressed
12:30 p.m.	Chris & Co. are served lunch	Venue delivers to room

	Lunch arrives for Pat's Party	ASAP Catering delivers
	Photographer leaves for venue	Photos for Chris' Party
	Florist arrives	Venue
1:30 p.m.	Limo arrives – Pat's house	Depart for venue
	Video crew arrives	Meet in lobby
2:30 p.m.	Pat Arrives w/Best Person	Venue
	Wedding Couple's "First Look" Photographer/Video Crew	Venue Ballroom

A complete list will include arrival times for the caterer, florist, baker, DJ, Musician, and Officiant. All vendors and their ETA will be listed here. Include the cocktail hour, scheduled dinnertime, the toasting, the cake cutting, first dance, DJ's end time.

(Sample Vendor List for the Wedding Day)

Vendor List for Chris and Pat's Wedding
June 15th

Role	Name	Contact
Role	**Name**	**Contact**
Day Of Coordinator	Molly	123.456.7890
Event Coordinator at Venue	Reese	123.456.7890
Officiant	Rev. Holly	123.456.7890
D.J.	Leslie/Best Ever DJ	123.456.7890
Photographer	Tanya/Frame It	123.456.7890
Hair	Megan/Salon	123.456.7890
Makeup	Whitney	123.456.7890
Wine Merchant	Char	123.456.7890
Oak Cellars	1983 Pinot Dr.	
Caterer	Lisa/Bites	123.456.7890
Florist	David/Gilded Lily	123.456.7890
Limo	John/Silver Ride	123.456.7890
Baker	Dan/Cakes & More	123.456.7890

Each of these vendors should be contacted 5 days before the wedding to confirm arrangements and be given any special instructions. Ideally, each vendor will have the "Day Of" Coordinator's name and phone number, along with directions to the venue. Bring to the rehearsal at least 3 sets of these Vendor Lists. One for "Day Of" Coordinator, one for Event Coordinator at venue and one is kept with the Wedding Couple, as backup.

EMERGENCY KIT LIST FOR YOUR WEDDING DAY

Labeling your belongings will increase the chance that they will be returned to you.

Tape:
Double Stick
Duct
Clear – Scotch tape in dispenser
Painter's Tape (comes in many colors now)
Tape gun loaded with fresh roll of clear packing tape

Extra Ribbon:
In wedding colors, any and a variety of widths

Sewing Kit:
Small, sharp scissors
GOOD Thread: white, black, gray, cream, Bridesmaid's dress colors
Safety pins – assorted sizes
Straight pins

Beauty/Toiletry:

Bobby pins	Deodorant	Kleenex
Hairspray	Tampons	Eye drops
Comb/brush	Mints/gum	Reading glasses
Mouthwash/floss	Lip balm	Clear nail polish

Plastic Bags:
Ziploc bags, assorted sizes
Several extra large black garbage bags
Smaller "kitchen size" draw string garbage bags

Office Supplies:
Three pair of scissors (make certain your name is on them)
Black permanent markers, fine point and larger
Post- it Notes – assorted sizes
White correction fluid or correction tape

Plain white copy paper – at least 25 sheets
Highlighters
Any extra paper for name tags, place cards of any kind – Blank, heavy stock
Black calligraphy pen – for signage
Glue and or glue stick
Stick pins: Clear and silver (heavy)
Black writing pens – at least 10
Legal pads – at least 2

Medical:

Band Aids, assorted sizes
Neosporin
Aspirin/Tylenol/Allergy medicine
Cough drops

Miscellaneous:

Rubber gloves

Cleaning cloths/dish towels
Small container of cleaning solution (Mr. Clean type of cleaner)
Fabric pen for cleaning stained white garments
Small bucket
Extra florist pins
Matches or butane clicker (long model)
Flashlight with fresh batteries
Extra NEW AA Batteries
Extension cords, all sizes
Electrical strip
Cell phone charger

Water/Snacks: Purchase enough bottled water for the wedding party and your families to have available during the photo shoot. Folks often get thirsty before caterers arrive, especially in hot weather. Pack granola bars. Vegies, fruit and sandwiches are great to have on hand.

Extra Directions: It is also a good idea for the "Day Of" Coordinator and Best Persons to have extra copies of directions to the venue in order to help guide guests that may be lost in route. Even with the new technology of navigator systems and Internet mapping tools, rural routes can be tricky.

Inspired Idea: Post-wedding, restock your "Emergency Kit" and loan these implements to your friends that are getting married. They will be truly grateful!

COMMUNITY CENTER/ RENTAL FACILITY GUIDELINES

If you are renting a community center or other rental venue, there will most likely be a contract with instructions for clean up. Make certain that you have extra copies of the contract and review with the community center what supplies they stock and what you are expected to provide. Clearly understand what needs to happen so that your *full* deposit is returned. Enlist a point person to recruit a "Team of Helpers" and coordinate the reception clean up. Friends may be willing to help but they will need guidance as to the expectations at the facility. This is not an easy task and it often happens late at night with fewer volunteers than originally committed.

❖ Make several copies of the original rental agreement, highlighting the clean up checklist. Include the name and phone number of your facility contact person, in case there are questions.

❖ Pack extra garbage bags, you may need them.

❖ Food containers, plastic wrap if extra food is being sent home with family.

❖ Bring extra vases – share flowers as a thank you to your helpers.

❖ Prepare a list of any items that need to be delivered back to florists, rental companies, and the Wedding Couple. Sometimes wedding gifts need to be transported securely.

❖ If there is a final inspection, make certain a family member or friend gets a copy of this report. In this way, you will have proof of the final inspection if there are issues later.

❖ Consider having your "Team of Helpers" take photos before the wedding setup. This will assist them when returning everything to its proper order. Take photos after cleanup. Great proof that it was completed according to instructions.

Officiant's Pre-Wedding Overview

❖ Be aware of all the laws regarding the legal documents for the Wedding Couple and how the paperwork needs to be completed. Most counties and parishes have websites detailing their specific regulations. Pay close attention to the laws of submission for the application and the wait period *prior* to the wedding. After the wedding, it is also an excellent idea to make plain copies of all paperwork for both the Officiant's file and for the Wedding Couple. The Officiant is usually responsible for filing the appropriate documents in a timely manner with the presiding county or parish after the wedding.

❖ On rare occasions, the Wedding Couple may insist on filing their own paperwork to the appropriate government agency. This is often done in military and immigration cases. In this case, the Officiant will make plain copies at the venue site: one set for Wedding Couple, one set for the Officiant's file. The Officiant will give the originals to the couple at the reception, with specific filing instructions. The couple should notify the Officiant when the filing has actually taken place so the Officiant is able to document this in his/her file.

❖ Either the Wedding Couple or the venue will determine the most suitable place for signing the legal documents following the ceremony. The Officiant reminds the selected witnesses (when applicable), where and when the signing of the legal documents will occur on the day of the wedding. Make certain to let the photographer and/or videographer know as well.

❖ Most couples embrace the idea of adjourning to a private room to sign their documents immediately following the ceremony. The Officiant joins the Wedding Couple, along with their chosen witnesses (when required by the state in which they are being married), and photographer/videographer. The Officiant brings the appropriate paperwork (filled out). Sometimes wine and food is set out. When the signing is completed, it is an ideal opportunity to leave the Wedding Couple for some intimate time to themselves. The Officiant can make sure that the room is cleared so they couple is able to be alone. This post ceremony "cuddle time" is a much-needed juncture for the Wedding Couple to recharge! Often times the Bride's dress is bustled after this break. *Warning: If paperwork is not signed immediately after the ceremony, it is a challenge to get all of the necessary participants corralled again!*

❖ Arrangements need to be made for a wireless lapel microphone for the Officiant if there will be more than 50 guests in attendance. If the wedding is to be held outside in a windy location, a sponge wind cover or a boom microphone may need to be on hand. It is also good to have a freestanding/or hand held microphone for the reader(s) or if the Wedding Couple would like to read something to one another.

❖ The Officiant should be informed if the Wedding Couple will NOT be seeing each other before the wedding. This way, the Officiant may assist with the logistics and the honoring of the separation. *It will be a more fun and relaxed day for the couple to see each other and for the photos to be taken before the wedding.*

❖ The Officiant may want to prepare and memorize a "Welcome Address" to the congregation. *Suggestions may be found under "Officiant's Welcome Address" on page 100.*

❖ A discussion between the Wedding Couple and Officiant regarding the start time of the actual wedding ceremony is prudent. If there is an expectation the wedding is to start punctually and there are unforeseeable issues, it creates a tense atmosphere before the wedding begins. To make a decision to allow the ceremony to start 5-10 minutes late may save undue anxiety. A more relaxed tone allows your guests to feel as if "all is well" upon their arrival.

❖ Since the First Member of the Wedding Couple is usually cloistered away with their attendants, it makes sense for the Second Member of the Wedding Couple to be in charge of giving the final nod as to the actual start time. Once in awhile, a significant family member is late because of bad weather or traffic. In this case, the Second

Member of the Wedding Couple makes the decision to delay the service further. The First Member of the Wedding Couple is informed and then an announcement is made to the guests that the wedding will be starting a bit late and thanking everyone for their patience. *Please see special instructions for "Best Person/Usher Overview for the Wedding Day" regarding head on page 127.*

❖ Permission from the Wedding Couple needs to be obtained so the Officiant may request that mobile phones be silenced at the beginning of the ceremony.

❖ The Officiant will discuss with the Wedding Couple his/her own style of "Pronouncing" the couple. Is this a quiet, final prayer or a dramatic "You are now Husband and Wife" or "Husband and Husband" or "Wife and Wife," loudly, for all to hear the proclamation?

❖ The Officiant will need to have the Wedding Couple decide if they want to be introduced as a newly married couple. If so, the choices are: "The Happy Couple" or "Chris and Pat Hudson" or the traditional "Mr. and Mrs. Chris Hudson." This is a great way to bring closure to the ceremony and cue the DJ to start the recessional music.

❖ Does a table need to be set up for a ritual – and who is requesting this from the rental company, venue or bringing one from home? Will it be draped and are there additional linens on the rental list?

❖ Review the Wedding Couple's Bio List, The Formal Escorting plans and The Processional scheme.

❖ If the Wedding Couple is choosing to incorporate a ritual, become familiar with the steps. *See instructions for the Unity Candle Ritual on page 99.*

❖ The Officiant will ask the Wedding Couple their preference regarding the releasing of their guests at the end of the ceremony. This takes place after the Recessional. The choices are either a "Verbal Release" or a "Formal Release." *Please see "After the Ceremony" under the "Best Person/Usher Overview for the Wedding Day" on page 131.*

UNITY CANDLE SERVICE

This rite will require a large pillar candle with holder, two tapered candles with holders and two votive candles with holders, a butane lighter and a table on which to place these items, preferably draped with a long linen. The large pillar candle should have been allowed to burn for one hour, so that it can be more easily lit at ceremony time. If this ritual is being done outside, there needs to be a hurricane lantern to shield it from a breeze. The two small votive candles will be lit before the actual ceremony. One unlit tapered candle is handed to each member of the Wedding Couple. They light them with the separate votive candles then bring their flames together over the larger unity candle and allow the joint flames to move slowly downward, together, towards the wick to light the Unity Candle. The lit tapered candles may be placed back in their holders. The Wedding Couple then moves back to their original position facing one another and holding hands. The attendant assigned to rearrange the train of the Bride's dress may need to take care of this again after the Bride returns into position. *The butane lighter should be kept nearby just in case candles lose their flame and a member of the wedding party needs to be appointed and ready to relight them if necessary.*

THE OFFICIANT'S WELCOME ADDRESS

Before the actual ceremony begins, it is an engaging practice for the Officiant to step from behind the Wedding Couple and personally greet the guests. A gracious commencement helps to make the guests feel comfortable and connected. It allows everyone to gently ease from their busy day into the sacredness of the proceedings.

The Welcome Address is a monologue that is ideally memorized. It should be brief, to the point, and specific to the Wedding Couple. Ideally this will be memorable and inspiring to the guests. It never includes personal details that would embarrass the couple. The secret to a fine delivery is to be prepared, efficient and genuine. Remember, this Address is not about the Officiant, it is about the Wedding Couple.

❖ This is an ideal time to ask for mobile phones to be turned off.

❖ Perhaps the Wedding Couple would like it mentioned that personal photos/videos are not to be taken during the service.

❖ If the ceremony start time is considerably later than planned, thank everyone again for their patience.

❖ Thank guests for making the Wedding Couple a priority in their busy lives.

❖ Mention the fact that some of the relatives and friends have traveled a great distance, when applicable.

❖ Memorize a quote that represents the Wedding Couple well.

❖ Tell a brief (and appropriate), story that exemplifies their love.

❖ It is the perfect opportunity to acknowledge the host the wedding is taking place in a private home.

❖ If it is a holiday, perhaps this would be incorporated that into the Welcome Address.

THE
REHEARSAL
SCHEME

WEDDING COUPLE'S REHEARSAL CHECKLIST

❖ Include the Ceremony Seating chart for the families of the Wedding Couple: at least three copies are needed: one for person in charge of tagging chairs, one for the Officiant, and the Wedding Couple keeps one copy as backup.

❖ Temporary nametags for family and participant's chairs (save pretty ones for wedding day). Post-it Notes work quite well for the rehearsal.

❖ Any reading(s) printed out, in large font and mounted on heavy paper for readers. Reading(s) are placed on reader's designated seat(s) before the rehearsal and brought back for the wedding day, and again placed on appropriate chair(s) for reader(s) prior to the wedding.

❖ Five sets of diagrams of The Formal Escorting and The Processional: one for Officiant, one for "Day Of" Coordinator, one for the Event Coordinator at the venue, one for DJ/Musicians and one for the Wedding Couple as backup.

❖ Ritual items.

❖ Ring pillow(s), flower basket(s), etc.

❖ All jewelry being used in the ceremony.

❖ Final payment for the Officiant (if applicable).

❖ Mock bridal bouquet made out of ribbon from bridal showers – used for practice.

❖ Legal documents to give to Officiant (if they have not already been delivered).

❖ Ceremony music and something to play the music on, if the timing of the processional is a concern.

❖ Driving directions to the post rehearsal meal (if necessary).

❖ Timelines - given to all family members, wedding party, and ceremony participants at the end of the rehearsal.

❖ Three sets of Vendor Lists: one for "Day Of" Coordinator, one for the Event Coordinator at the venue, one kept by the Wedding Couple as backup.

How to Organize and Conduct a Rehearsal

A rehearsal is suggested if you are having *any* attendants whatsoever. The purpose of this practice session is to polish the details of the actual wedding ceremony so that the entire wedding party knows what is expected of them. To practice these formal logistics, is to insure a seamless service. This is also an opportunity for friends and family to meet and mingle. A walk-through truly helps to put nerves at ease and assures that everyone enjoys a better night's sleep!

Setting the Date and Time of the Rehearsal

First of all, make certain that the Officiant is available! Most venues DO NOT wish to schedule rehearsals on Friday late afternoons or evenings because they are hoping to rent that space for another event. So the typical rehearsal times are: Wednesday evenings, Thursday during the day or evening and Friday during the day.

Hosting a meal following a rehearsal is optional. And if you are having a rehearsal meal, sometimes a lunch works well. It leaves the evening open to accomplish last minute details. If family or attendants are making a time zone adjustment, it gives them the opportunity to rest.

When scheduling the rehearsal, be sensitive about the time of day you set, as several people may be traveling or working. Holiday and special event traffic should be considered.

If someone in your wedding party is unable to attend, your Officiant might be willing to do a quick walk through on the wedding day with the missing participants.

Who needs to be present at the rehearsal?

- ❖ The Officiant
- ❖ "Day Of" Coordinator
- ❖ Escort(s) for either (or both) of the Wedding Couple (if applicable)
- ❖ Wedding party: "Best People" standing up with the Wedding Couple (including flower girls, ring bearers)

Nice to have in attendance, but optional:

❖ Parents, grandparents of the Wedding Couple, stepparent(s) and step grandparent(s)
❖ Sibling(s) of the Wedding Couple
❖ Readers (readers should have been sent their reading prior to the wedding)
❖ Ushers

DO NOT need to be present:

❖ DJ/Musicians
❖ Photographers
❖ Video team

A well-orchestrated rehearsal should take about an hour (providing everyone arrives on time).

The wedding couple should NOT be conducting the rehearsal themselves. *A third party ideally carries out this task. The Officiant or the "Day Of" coordinator would be best suited. Hereafter, this designated person will be referred to as the "PRR" (Person Running the Rehearsal).*

INSPIRED SUGGESTION

Make arrangements with your venue to arrive at least one half hour earlier than the other rehearsal attendees. This is an ideal time to take care of event details. Sometimes chairs must to be set up for the rehearsal. (You'll need at least two rows on each side, with five or six chairs in each row with a "2-3 person wide" aisle in between.) Ask the Event Coordinator at your venue if they are willing to store your wedding décor, programs, party favors, signage, guest book - and anything else you want delivered early. This also gives you a chance to meet with your Officiant give her/him the rings and review your scheme.

Please note: *These detailed instructions are for the Second Member of the Wedding Couple walking in earlier, and the First Member of the Wedding Couple making a grand entrance with all guests standing to honor them. This guide may be easily modified according to your specific wishes and plans. Amend away!*

Before the Rehearsal Begins

Make sure the chairs that have been set up for the rehearsal have temporary nametags for both the family and ceremony participants according to the VIP Ceremony Seating chart. (Post-it Notes work well.) This will help everyone have a clear idea of where they will be anchored for the actual ceremony and will save much confusion on the wedding day.

The PRR will give the mock bouquet(s) to the Bride(s) and collect the wedding rings to be used at the service. The PRR will give the Second Member of the Wedding Couple's ring to the MOH/Best Person and the First Member of the Wedding Couple's ring to the Best Man/Person. The flower girls and ring bearers will be given their props as well. Any ritual items will need to be set up appropriately at the front Altar Area (perhaps on a table), so that the Wedding Couple will be able to practice.

Preliminary Walk-Through With the Wedding Couple's Escort(s)

Practicing with the Wedding Couple's escort(s) before the rehearsal allows this core group a chance to get the choreography well orchestrated. The Officiant or the PRR takes the place of the First Member of the Wedding Couple for this "trial run." They will stand where the wedding party will enter to make their *slow* walk down the aisle. In a perfect scenario, the Best Person/MOH will be in position at the Altar Area (just a few feet to the right of the Officiant as they face the entrance), and the Second Member of the Wedding Couple will be standing to the Officiant's left at the Altar Area facing the direction of the entrance.

The PRR will describe to the escort(s) that the tempo is like a SLOW and relaxed walk in the park. They will explain to the escort(s) that there are *TWO* distinct cues for the escort(s) to know just before they walk down the aisle:

1. First, the music will change to the Wedding Couple's selection of her/his grand entrance song.

2. Then the Officiant will have everyone stand prior to the First Member of the Wedding Couple entering by saying, "All rise."

The PRR (standing in for First Member of the Wedding Couple) takes the escort's right arm. This taking of the right arm keeps the escort from being wedged between the Wedding Couple during the hand-off at the Altar Area.

If two escorts are involved, they should find a comfortable solution regarding who will be taking which arms.

After the PRR and the escort(s) take their slow walk down the aisle towards the Altar Area, they will stop at the first row of chairs. When a bouquet is in the scheme, the Best Person/MOH will step forward and take the bouquet and return to her/his appointed spot. The First Member of the Wedding Couple and escort(s) will have a moment to hug, and then the Second Member of the Wedding Couple will step forward, first shaking the hand or hugging the escort(s).

Now the Wedding Couple will be holding hands and will stand directly in front of the Officiant, facing one another. At this point the escort(s) walk(s) back to their designated seat(s).

Suggested Etiquette: If groomsmen are paired with bridesmaids in the processional, they will be escorting the women with their left arms during the processional and right arms during the recessional. If it is a mixed group of males and females on each side — let etiquette be relaxed and just make a plan that works for all.

Beginning a Rehearsal: First Staging

Please see the diagram titled "First Staging: The Beginning of The Rehearsal" on page 119.

Before starting the rehearsal the PRR will check with the Wedding Couple to make sure that everyone is present and ask permission for the rehearsal to begin.

When it is time to start the rehearsal, the PRR will introduce herself/himself and clearly state: "Welcome — the rehearsal is NOW beginning." Then the PRR will instruct the family members and wedding participants to be seated in their tagged chairs. The PRR will then line up all the attendants, in what we will refer to as the Altar Area (where the ceremony will take place), in their appropriate positions as detailed in the Processional diagram. The PRR will call out the names of the attendants, starting with the attendant standing closest to the Second Member of the Wedding Couple. The PRR will clearly show each of them where they will be standing during the wedding ceremony. With this target zone identified, there is no confusion when the wedding party arrives back to the Altar Area after completing the processional for the first time.

The same exercise is repeated for First Member of the Wedding Couple's side.

When the Best People are positioned, the PRR will ask the Wedding Couple to introduce their families and attendants.

In a respectful show of support the Wedding Couple will stand near the PRR or Officiant while the following items are reviewed:

❖ Instruct everyone to stay for the Wedding Day Timelines that will be handed out at the *end* of the rehearsal. (If Timelines are given out at the beginning of the rehearsal the entire focus may be lost.)

❖ State that the wedding party is present to support the Wedding Couple and their families with whatever task may be needed on the big day. Being ready and willing to serve is essential.

❖ The Ushers/Best Persons are to meet in the entrance "lobby" area where the ceremony is to take place one half hour before the wedding begins, to be given last minute instructions before welcoming guests and helping them to their seats.

❖ Request that no member of the wedding party is to leave the venue site without first informing the Officiant or "Day Of" Coordinator. Explain that you will have an emergency kit on the premises and let them know whom to contact for access. *Please see list of suggestions for "Emergency Kit List for Your Wedding Day" on page 92.*

❖ Enlighten the wedding party as to the exact locations of the bathrooms. As attendants, they may be asked this question on the day of the wedding.

❖ Encourage the wedding party to eat healthy meals and drink plenty of water on the day of the wedding. Many weddings have been ruined by guests of all ages becoming dehydrated and needing hospitalization. Alcohol should be minimized, as attendants are sometimes asked to run an errand on the wedding day. Gently remind everyone that the ceremony is a time of decorum and that we are all making treasured memories for the Wedding Couple.

❖ Remind everyone to bring a comfortable pair of shoes to the wedding — most women's high heels and men's rented shoes become painful after a few hours.

The Processional:

The PRR now demonstrates/discusses the following:

❖ Explain to everyone that the actual rehearsal begins at the end of the ceremony so that everyone is aware of their target position. Explain that the processional is the walking in of the wedding party and the recessional is the exit. Clarify that you will begin the rehearsal by fast forwarding to the end of service, practicing the recessional and then lining up for the processional, followed by the run through of the ceremony with another recesional.

❖ How the female Best Persons will walk down the aisle: heads up, bouquets at waist, slow pace, and smile!

❖ Male attendants must have sunglasses off, hands out of pockets and standing with their hands folded in front or hands by their sides, whichever the Wedding Couple prefers. (Hands clasped behind backs create a gap in the jackets.)

❖ If male attendants are escorting the female attendants, the fellows will make a gentle fist with their hands at their waists with their elbow held close to their bodies. The female Best Persons will slide their hand into that small space at the elbow.

❖ If attendants are walking in by pairs during the processional, they need to rehearse how to separate once they arrive at the Altar Area. They will glance at one another just before turning to proceed to their designated positions. This makes for a more courteous separation, versus the awkward dropping of the arm and stiffly walking to positions.

❖ Instruct the wedding party as they are standing at the Altar Area to face the aisle and then slowly shift their bodies as the First Member of the Wedding Couple makes her/his way up to the Altar Area — always facing towards the person making the grand entrance - similar to a sunflower to the sun!

❖ *The Officiant will now quickly practice the ending of the service.* The Wedding Couple is positioned in front of the Officiant, facing one another and holding hands. They are prompted to have a kiss. At this time the Officiant gracefully steps out of the frame of any photos that will be taken at the end of the actual ceremony and stand near the Best Person. The Wedding Couple is asked to then face their guests. If there is/are flower bouquet(s) involved in this sequence, the Officiant instructs the Best Person/MOH to step around to the front of the Wedding Couple to hand back the bouquet(s). The Officiant will then introduce the Wedding Couple as either "The Happy Couple" or "Chris and Pat Hudson" or the traditional "Mr. and Mrs. Chris Hudson." This is when the Officiant asks everyone to clap.

❖ The Wedding Couple will turn to face their guests and pause for photos to be taken. Their Recessional song will begin to play then they slowly walk down the aisle. During the rehearsal, the Officiant may remind them where they will be going after the real wedding ceremony to sign the legal documents, "Remember to meet me in the Board Room to sign the paperwork."

❖ When the Wedding Couple walks all the way down the main aisle, the Best Persons meet in the center of the Altar Area and the Best Person offers his/her arm. The next couple will exit, when the Best Persons are about halfway down the main aisle. The rest of the wedding party will exit in the same fashion. If there are two males or two females exiting together, they do not need to take an arm unless this is their preference.

PRACTICING THE FORMAL ESCORTING, THE PROCESSIONAL AND THE RECESSIONAL: SECOND STAGING

Please see to the Diagram titled "Second Staging for Rehearsal: Lining Up of Family and Wedding Party" on page 120.

The PRR will instruct everyone to meet in the area where they will be lining up to enter. The PRR will line up the wedding party and family according to the Formal Escorting and the Processional diagrams prepared by the Wedding Couple. Since this group was shown their seats at the very beginning of the rehearsal, they should be well aware of their target chair or the place that they will be standing at the Altar Area. The escorts, especially children and grandchildren, are instructed to give their parents and grandparents a hug and or kiss when they arrive at their designated seat. The family will sit down when they arrive at their appointed chair. They will be standing again when the Officiant says, "All rise" when the First Member of the Wedding Couple makes their grand entrance.

Depending on the length of the walk to arrive at the Altar Area and the music selected, the pacing needs to be determined. If it is a lengthy walk, attendants need to be spaced so huge gaps do not occur. Some songs may need to be looped by the DJ. If live music has been arranged, professional musicians are able to repeat quite easily.

If the Second Member of the Wedding Couple is escorting his/her mother (which is such a charming practice) the Officiant will arrive up front before this member of the Wedding Couple, so that they are not standing at the Altar Area alone. Instruct members of the wedding party that will be escorting more than one person, to circle back along the side aisle and stand with their second charge. Example: Sometimes the escort/parent walks his/her wife/ partner down the center aisle and returns, (using a side aisle), to the entrance area to escort one of the members of the Wedding Couple.

The PRR will begin sending everyone involved in the formal escorting and the processional down the center aisle towards the Altar Area, instructing everyone about the appropriate spacing between the parties.

Since the wedding party has already been shown their intended positions at the Altar Area, they should know exactly what target space they occupy when arriving up front.

When children are involved in the wedding processional, they will walk to the front and will be greeted by the Officiant and then directed to their designated seats. Ring bearers hand their pillows (or containers), to the Officiant at this time. Flower girls will take their baskets to their seats with them. Any child under the age of nine typically lacks the attention span to stand up front for 20 to 30 minutes. Remember that these children are attending an adult function. They frequently become bored and start acting out. It is best to allow them to sit (ideally with a quiet activity waiting at their designated seats).

Now it is time for the First Member of the Wedding Couple to make her/his grand entrance. With the parent(s) seated in the appropriate chairs and the wedding party in their designated places, the Officiant will direct everyone with her/his arms in an upswing motion saying, "All rise please" while looking at the parent(s) of the Wedding Couple for leadership.

The First Member of the Wedding Couple and their escort(s) will slowly enter and walk down the aisle. The "hand off" between the First Member of the Wedding Couple and the escort will happen as previously described. The Officiant will say, "You may be seated" to the entire congregation, again looking to the parents for leadership. The Officiant will now run through the ceremony.

If the reader is present, they are instructed to come forward and stand so that they are facing the Wedding Couple. The Wedding Couple will face the reader. The reader does not need to actually perform the reading at the rehearsal. Just have them say the words, "Blah, blah, blah."

The Officiant will not be reading the entire wedding - just the important highlights. The Vows should be kept private until the actual wedding day, so they are not practiced at the rehearsal. The logistics for any Ritual chosen for the service would be practiced at this time.

The Officiant will recite out loud the Ring Exchange. In practicing the Ring Exchange, the Officiant walks over to the Best Persons to collect the rings and returns to face the Wedding Couple. The Second Member of the Wedding Couple is handed the ring that they will be giving to their sweetheart. The First Member of the Wedding Couple is instructed to drop her/his right hand so that the only hand available on which to place a ring is their left hand. The Second Member of the Wedding Couple places one of his/her hands under their sweetheart's hand and slides the ring just to the second knuckle of the ring finger and stops there. The Officiant will then begin reciting the Vow Exchange (in small phrases), with the Second Member of the Wedding Couple repeating the words. When finished, the Officiant will whisper the word,

"Perfect" as a cue for them to slide the ring all the way onto their sweetheart's finger. The Officiant will now hand the second ring to the First Member of the Wedding Couple as their sweetheart drops his/her right hand leaving their left hand palm side down for the First Member of the Wedding Couple to slide the ring onto the ring finger – stopping at the second knuckle. Again, the Officiant speaks a few phrases at a time of the Ring Exchange with the First Member of the Wedding Couple following the Officiant's lead. And again the Officiant whispers the word, "Perfect" so the First Member of the Wedding Couple knows to continue sliding the ring onto their sweetheart's finger. Following the Ring Exchange, the Wedding Couple continues holding hands, facing one another. Please note: So the intimacy of the Wedding Couple is maintained, they may repeat the words after the Officiant at any volume. On the actual wedding day, the guests will hear the words because the Officiant is either projecting well (for a smaller group), or is wired with a decent lapel microphone (guests of 50+).

The Officiant will move ahead to the end of the ceremony that was rehearsed previously:
- ❖ The Pronouncement
- ❖ The Kiss
- ❖ Bouquet handed back by the Best Person
- ❖ Introduction of the Wedding Couple
- ❖ Recessional

Any seated children that were involved in the processional, are nudged to exit at this time. If they are not in the mood to participate, allow them to remain seated. *Note: It is a compassionate deed to assign any single parent an escort for the recessional. A member of the wedding party may have escorted them in and this leaves them without an escort for the exit. Often times an uncle or auntie can be assigned.*

The entire wedding party meets again in the foyer or entrance area and lines up. Allow them to queue up for the processional on their own, without direction. The PRR will check to make sure that everyone is in the proper places according to the Formal Escorting/ Processional diagrams. Another quick run-through of the formal escorting, processional and ceremony takes place.

ADDITIONAL DETAILS:

❖ Be aware of any special announcements that the Officiant needs to make at the end of the service that will help streamline the reception. Ask the Event Coordinator at the venue what final announcements they would like made. Does the room need to be emptied so the staff is able to reset it for dinner? Where do you want the guests to reconvene? Are there special family photos that need to be taken after the wedding and would an announcement be helpful? Make sure that the DJ/Music Person is informed if announcements need to be made so that the music is quieted.

❖ Request that at least one parent of the ring bearer(s) and flower girl(s) stay with the wedding party as the group queues up on the wedding day. This is wise if there is a need for bathroom visits or behavior issues arise. The parent can quietly enter down the side aisle and take their seat after their child has made their entry. This assures that the wedding party is not babysitting the children.

❖ Let the wedding party know that the landscape for the center aisle and the Altar Area may be quite different on the day of the wedding. Arches, pillars, urns, drapes and tables magically appear.

❖ If there is a longer train on the bride's dress, one of the attendants is asked to be the stylist and rearrange the train once the bride is in place at the Altar Area. The train is lifted a few inches above the floor and waved so that air is brought into the fabric and easier to handle. It is then draped around the back and "puddles" towards the front. In this way, it will look attractive in the photos.

The "Timeline for the wedding Day" is given to the wedding party and families before everyone leaves the rehearsal. Ideally the "Day Of" Coordinator allows time for the group to review it and will answer questions. This will minimize confusion of the wedding day. The "Vendor List" is handed out to appropriate parties at this time. Driving directions might be given out as well, if there is a meal following the rehearsal.

First Staging

The Beginning of the Rehearsal

Front Altar Area

Note: You will actually begin the rehearsal by re-enacting the very end of the ceremony. All family members, ceremony participants and attendants will be placed in the position from which they will be observing the actual ceremony. This gives everyone their "target zone." They will clearly understand where to sit/stand after the processional.

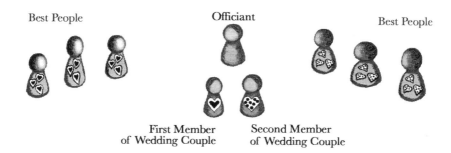

Best People   Officiant   Best People

First Member of Wedding Couple   Second Member of Wedding Couple

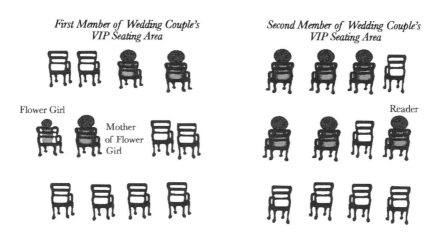

First Member of Wedding Couple's VIP Seating Area   *Second Member of Wedding Couple's VIP Seating Area*

Flower Girl

Mother of Flower Girl

Reader

Second Staging for Rehearsal

Lining up the Family and Wedding Party

Front Altar Area

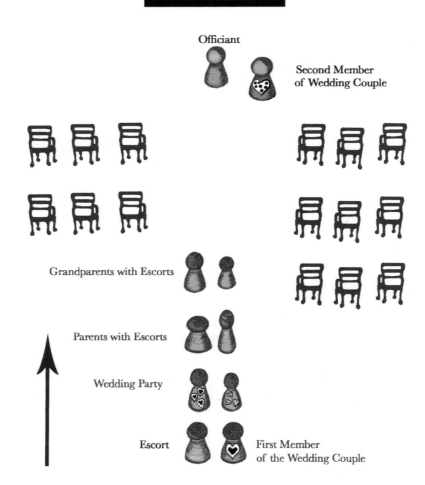

Officiant

Second Member of Wedding Couple

Grandparents with Escorts

Parents with Escorts

Wedding Party

Escort

First Member of the Wedding Couple

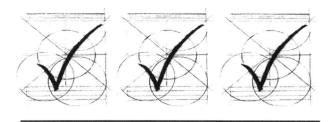

"DAY OF"
CHECKLISTS

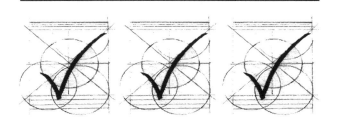

Ceremony Checklist for The Wedding Couple for the Wedding Day:

In a perfect world, most of these items would have been delegated to appropriate persons or delivered to the designated places prior to the wedding day.

- ❖ Legal documents (given to Officiant)

- ❖ VIP name tags/chart (given to designated helper)

- ❖ Rings – all jewelry needed for ceremony

- ❖ Final Payments/Tips for Vendors, prepared and in envelopes, to be given to "Day Of" Coordinator or Best Person to distribute

- ❖ Ritual items, Unity Candle Set, etc. need to be handed to "Day Of" Coordinator so she/he doesn't have to go in search of them

- ❖ Flower girl baskets, ring pillows – or other items the children in the processional will be carrying

- ❖ Emergency Kit

- ❖ Snacks and bottled water for wedding party

- ❖ VIP Ceremony Seating Chart/Tags

OFFICIANT'S WEDDING DAY CHECKLIST

❖ The Wedding Couple's personal ceremony should be printed out in large font, typically three-hole punched and placed in an attractive three ring binder. It might be helpful for the Officiant to have notes written directly on these pages and pause marks made with highlighters. The Officiant, by this time, should be very familiar with this particular ceremony. Warning: Often the venue dims the lighting and it is hard to read in this lovely *ambiance*! Reading glasses and a flashlight may be helpful.

❖ The Officiant's Welcome Address, notes, quotes.

❖ Bring several copies of diagrams of Formal Escorting/Processional, depending on who may still need them. Day of Coordinator, DJ/Musicians and Event Coordinator at the venue, as well as the Officiant all need a set. Officiant places his/her copy in the front of their ceremony binder along with the Wedding Couple's Bio List.

❖ Extra copies of any Reading(s) or Vows, Writings that will be read by the Wedding Couple or readers during the service, printed and mounted on heavy stock. Readings will be placed on the reader's chairs at the ceremony. Vows/Writings are kept in Officiant's binder ready to hand to the Wedding Couple (if they are reading), at the appropriate time during the ceremony. If one of the attendants is doing a reading, their copy is handed to them during the service.

❖ Kleenex folded neatly and kept in the ceremony binder (for the Wedding Couple, if there are tears).

❖ Legal documents filled out and ready to sign.

❖ Comfortable shoes — some venues are spread out and there is a great deal of walking on hard services, muddy paths and wet fields. Change into your fancier wedding shoes prior to the start of the ceremony.

❖ Pack a *good* pen that writes well and looks decent in photographs. Keep it handy for signing of the legal documents.

❖ VIP Ceremony Seating Chart that the Wedding Couple has prepared placed in front of binder.

❖ Extra blank seating charts, (just in case this detail was overlooked by the Wedding Couple).

❖ The first page of the binder will include a checklist of everything that the Officiant must do before the ceremony. *Please see "Officiant's Wedding Day Task List" on page 125.*

In a seasoned Officiant's binder, they will have a "pencil pocket" in the back filled with folded Kleenex, mints, scissors, extra plain name cards (just in case), clear tape, Post-it Notes and extra pens.

Officiant's Wedding Day Task List

The Officiant arrives at least one hour before the wedding.

❖ Meets with the DJ/Musicians; possibly gives them diagrams for the formal escorting and processional.

❖ Seldom will DJ's/Musicians attend the rehearsal, so the Officiant gives them instructions on the "looped" music along with the Formal Escorting/Processional diagrams. When appropriate, the Officiant will also be wired at this time with the microphone and test the sound system for all microphones. Thorough testing of the wireless equipment is necessary as this bandwidth is widely used and there may be interference.

❖ If possible, the Officiant does another walk-through with flower girls, ring bearers, grandparents and any members of the wedding party that were not present at the rehearsal.

❖ The Officiant would be wise to check the nametags on the VIP chairs. Don't hesitate to ask the Wedding Couple's parent(s) to check them as well. They are familiar with this group and will know if something is askew.

❖ The Officiant makes sure that the grandparents know where to sit following their entrance. This task can easily be delegated to the Wedding Couple's parents.

❖ The Officiant will collect the wedding rings and give them to the Best Persons.

❖ The Officiant will also inform the photographer, video team and witnesses when and where the legal documents will be signed.

❖ Meet with the reader(s), give them instructions, allow them to test the microphone and make sure the hard copy of the reading is placed on the reader's designated seat(s).

❖ The Officiant will remind the Best Persons to make sure that each member of the Wedding Couple visits their respective bathrooms about 20 minutes before start time and have mints available.

❖ Ideally the Officiant will check to see that all props for any Ritual are in place at the Altar Area and that the flower baskets and ring pillows are in the entrance area.

❖ The Officiant will then meet with the Best Persons/Ushers to give last minute instructions and explain any changes. Seating of guests will begin about 20 minutes before start time. *Please see "Best Person/Usher Overview for the Wedding Day" on page 127.*

❖ If she/he has not done so before, the Officiant will ask the venue staff about any announcements needing to be made before the guests are released following the ceremony.

BEST PERSON/USHER OVERVIEW FOR THE WEDDING DAY

Ushers/Best Persons, Best Person/Man and possibly one member of the Wedding Couple gather one half hour prior to the wedding start time to help greet and seat the guests. The Wedding Couple's parents make fine greeters as well.

Counting Guests

As time draws closer for the ceremony to begin, it is a great asset to have a guest head count. One of the Ushers/Best Persons will be assigned to do a guest calculation. To arrive at this calculation subtract the number of people in the Formal Escorting and the Processional from the final guest count (guests that sent an RSVP). This will give you the number of actual *seated* guests that you will be expecting. Then count the total number of guest chairs set up in the wedding ceremony area. The total number of expected seated guests is subtracted from total number of chairs in the room. *This will be your empty chair count.* As the time draws closer to the start of the wedding – all the "Counter" has to do is track the number of empty chairs to know when all expected guests have arrived. When there is a significant number of an empty chair nearing the start time, the Wedding Couple and Officiant will need to be informed so a decision can be made to delay the start time of the ceremony.

Example:	Final Guest Count:	125
	Less wedding party and family in Formal Escorting/Processional	10
	Actual seated guests (when they all arrive):	115
	Total chairs in room: (extras are typically set up)	135
	Less seated guests:	115
	Empty/extra chairs:	20
	(The ideal situation is to be counting 20 empty chairs at start time)	

Example based on this scenario: It is close to start time and there are 50 empty chairs – you know that there are about 30 guests missing and the ceremony should be delayed.

Be sure to keep the Event Coordinator of the venue aware of the decision to delay the ceremony, as this will affect the timing of the food preparation. A message should be sent to the Wedding Couple and Families as well.

Seating Families with Small Children and the Designated Bouncer of Disruptive Children

Either the Usher or the Best Person standing furthest from the members of the Wedding Couple (during the ceremony), has the task of leaving to escort a crying/disruptive child and their parent(s) away from the ceremony. This keeps the Officiant from having to interrupt the service and embarrass the disruptive family. Instruct the Usher/Best Person to escort the family to a place where they can no longer be heard. A bathroom with closed doors works rather well. The Usher/Best Person will assist the family with anything they may need and then returns to be seated (Usher), or stand with the wedding party (Best Person).

When seating a family with young children, the magical phrase is, "These seats closest to the door might be best for you just in case your children become vocal and need to be taken out." This gives the parents a strong message of the expected protocol.

If a white aisle runner is laid down in the center aisle at the ceremony site Ushers/Best Persons will escort guests to their seats from the side aisles. Have guests "snuggle up" so empty chairs are not in between them.

Escorting

In a less formal setting, the guests can be led towards the wedding seating area and instructed to find their own seats. With a more formal wedding (or with plenty of Ushers/Best Persons), guests may be guided towards the front, and directed to available seats. If the

Ushers/Best Persons are male, they might offer their left arm to a female guest and males usually follow. If Ushers are women, they simply walk in front or along side the guest(s) and may indicate (with a palm up motion), where guests are to be seated.

Guests that arrive early typically like to gather and chat. The larger the wedding, the longer it takes to get friends and family seated. Allow approximately 20 minutes to help 100 people to their seats, depending on the cooperation of the group and whether a bar is open for serving beverages. If a bar is open for a pre-function, allow additional time for seating. As the wedding gets closer to the scheduled start time, the Ushers/Best Persons need to be more determined in guiding people to their seats. Some guests may be dedicated "Beehivers" and stay huddled together, deep in conversation.

The VIP nametags will have been placed on the chairs in the reserved VIP Ceremony Seating Area by the time the Ushers/Best Persons start seating guests. This reduces confusion and clearly designates the VIP territory.

Typically Ushers/Best Persons will not ask guests on which side they prefer to be seated when showing guests to their seats. "Side Specific" guest counts may vary dramatically resulting in an imbalance of seated guests. The "mixed guest" method is more practical. It is best to begin seating guests behind the VIP Seating Area, towards the front.

ADDITIONAL TIPS:

- ❖ The Ushers/Best Persons need to know the exact locations of the bathrooms so that they are able to direct guests.

- ❖ Ushers/Best Persons should be sensitive to guests arriving in wheel chairs. Ushers will remove a side aisle chair where the wheel chair will be placed. This extra guest chair is often placed in the entry area for elderly family members that need to sit before they walk down the aisle during the formal escorting. In fact, several chairs for the elderly may need to be brought to the waiting area where the bridal party is gathering.

- ❖ Ushers/Best Persons may want to remind guests to sign some kind of guest registry. Ushers/Best Persons may hand out programs and inform guests where to place their gifts and cards. If the line for signing the registry becomes too long and it is time to begin the service, guests may be asked to return to complete this activity at the cocktail hour or reception.

- ❖ If there are designated Ushers, they ideally will stand near the back of the ceremony room *after* the ceremony has started to help with both latecomers finding seats and parents of crying babies.

One of the members of the Wedding Couple will be the point person deciding when the wedding ceremony begins. *Frequently one party of the Wedding Couple remains "hiding" and one will be meeting and greeting guests in the entrance area.*

AFTER THE CEREMONY

The Verbal Release vs. The Formal Release of the Wedding Guests

For the "Verbal Release," the Officiant simply announces that they will be releasing the first row of the First Member of the Wedding Couple's family (using her/his name), then releasing the first row the Second Member of the Wedding Couple's family (using his/her name).

The Wedding Couple may choose to do a "Formal Release" following the recessional. This is when the two Best Persons doubling as Ushers (after escorting any attendants back down the center aisle), return to the Altar Area. The Ushers stand near the two front aisle chairs on either side of the center aisle. They wait until the Officiant is finished making any announcements and the Usher facing the family located in front left side, as you face the Altar Area, bows slightly and motions with his/her left hand, indicating that it is now time for this family to exit down the center aisle. As this row, on the left side empties, the Usher on the right side of the aisle bows slightly to this VIP front row indicating it is now time for this family to exit. Then the other Usher releases the left side, second row. The rows are emptied in turn, going back and forth as the Ushers work their way down the center aisle.

HAPPILY
EVER AFTER

Quick Guide for a Balanced Marriage

Marriage is the art of being in service, in sync and in love - all at the same time. Here's a gentle guide to help you foster an enduring partnership.

And please know, that this guide is a condensed read. Many in-depth books have been written on every aspect of relationships. This is just one small resource.

On Humbleness and Gratitude

Try to say something supportive and loving to your spouse every day. Notice the little things that he or she does for you and say thank you. You will never be faulted for being too appreciative!

Keep your ego in check. We all transition through pockets of self-absorption. Be aware of this temporary phase and acknowledge it to your partner.

It is quite charming when someone is humble enough to admit when they are wrong. Have you ever noticed that the sooner one admits their mistake the easier it is to forgive them? Genuinely ask for forgiveness. *Accountability, absolution and compromise are the cornerstones to long and happy relationships.*

Try not to offer yourself up as a stellar example of perfection. If you need to make a suggestion or request - be gentle.

You really do not want to "win" every disagreement. It will sabotage *any* relationship. Healthy adult disagreements end with each party taking responsibility and sharing their resolve to change their behavior(s). "Winning" is very much an ego-based conduct. Be mindful of the power struggles. They are minefields.

Be willing to find win-win solutions!

On Romance

As silly as this may sound, eventually you will need to take time to plan romance. It is essential that you schedule time to talk, play and even have sex. Life gets busy and our priorities unconsciously shift.

Plan a date night at least once a week, without children, friends, relatives or phones. Take turns planning and organizing the date. It should be mutually enjoyable. Adopt the wise rule to NOT discuss household business during this time. Take this time to validate and nurture your partner.

Tell your spouse daily that you love them. Be affectionate frequently. Write notes, leave messages, and be thoughtful and surprising.

Laughter is a balm. Don't let the art of flirting get rusty. Remember to PLAY, tease and giggle. Having fun together will keep you young and the marriage vital.

Be aware that our definition of romance will change with time. Sometimes it might be cooking a nice dinner for your sweetheart. It may be encouraging them to go play golf or have lunch with girlfriends. Romance may be fixing something in need of repair around your home – or hiring a repairperson. Eventually it might be doing something kind for your partner's parents.

Intimacy is a barometer to any marriage. It is found in communication, in affection, in a glance, in a trusted confidence. It is reflected in sexual relations.

When we take the time to rekindle and renew our marriage, it will pay great dividends!

On Being Roommates

Being a good roommate means you've developed a balanced set of ethics. Fairness is a key ingredient in a solid marriage.

Pay attention when somebody tells you that things are not quite equal.

❖ Is the cleaning of the house and doing the laundry shared?
❖ Are both of you helping to pay bills, resolving account issues, and preparing paper-work for the IRS?
❖ Who is participating in the holiday errands and tasks?
❖ Are you a team primping the house and cooking when you entertain? Are you both cleaning up after guests leave?
❖ Who is tracking the auto maintenance? Does this count as a household chore?
❖ If one is cooking, is the other one cleaning up?

We each have our own priorities. Just make sure that you are hearing your partner about the ethics of helping! Be in agreement with just what the actual chore is - as well as how frequently it needs to be accomplished. This will keep the molehills from becoming mountains.

Resentment is the direct result of imbalance.
And resentment is a bitter toxin to rid from any marriage.

Be mindful when you are justifying certain behaviors or shirking responsibilities. Try to divvy up the nastiest of tasks. It is common for each of the partners to see the duties in the marriage as unequal. You can, however, be aware of how much each of you are contributing...especially if this issue of imbalance keeps arising! And then equalize the chore chart.

Compassion goes a long way to resolve these negotiations. Empathy will make you an easier person with whom to live. To be fair, is not only saying the words. It is putting into action the promises that you've made. Helping your loved one to unburden the heavy responsibility will make you look like a hero.

A healthy marriage fosters the theory that the roles are flexible and turns are taken with the unpleasant duties. Added bonus: He or she may find it sexy!

Brilliant Idea: When one of you decides to undertake a significant project, allow that person the leadership role. They can be called the "general" of the project. This makes the other partner the "corporal." In this way, it keeps the project moving ahead with reduced interference from the less involved party. For example: Sarah was cleaning the deck and her partner came along to offer *loads* of advice on cleaners and scrapers. Like a good general, she took some of the advice but finished the project in the manner that best suited her. Her partner respected her decisions.

Financial earnings should not be used to control household or partnership issues. For example: Pat wouldn't tell Chris that Pat didn't have to help with household chores because Pat earned more money. But if Chris was a "stay-at-home parent" and has more time at home than Pat, it would be fair for Chris to take on more of the household tasks.

On Being Aware of Moods

Sometimes we get cranky and don't know why. This isn't fun for you or for your sweetheart. Be aware of your moods and the "why" of them. If you are feeling depressed, don't have somebody else deliver the news to you. Take time to know your feelings and examine why they are with you. Develop the trust and wisdom to share your fears, concerns, and stresses with your spouse. Explain to them your struggles and share your discoveries. And hopefully your spouse will appreciate your vulnerability and be relieved that you are aware of your issues.

Your partner may have some inspired insights and suggestions to share with you. Usually with this kind of vulnerability, your spouse will have compassion and patience.

Be willing to ask your partner for what you reasonably need and want. This may be social, physical, emotional, financial or spiritual in nature. Your husband or wife is not a mind reader. They need to know what you need.

Discuss the possibilities. Dream a little. And do your best to help make it happen.

Schedule time to foster peace and harmony within yourself.

Have quiet time and take a deep breath. Become stewards of one another's tranquility. Be mindful of the amount of calm you bring to the union as well as the drama and tension you generate.

So take time to mediate, pray, reflect and set intentions. These will become your compasses in life.

It is helpful for all of us to track our thoughts, feelings, and progress in overcoming challenges in a journal. It is a tangible way to measure improvements and gain insight into behaviors.

Many insightful books are available. Begin the tradition of reading to one another.

Trick Question: Are you being the kind of partner to whom you want to be married?

Setting Personal Intentions

Adopting positive habits and shifting unwanted patterns needs to be a conscious venture. And you don't have to wait until next January! It is believed that if you are able to maintain your new intentions for 21 days, you have an excellent chance of success.

❖ Begin by writing down your Intentions. Start with a few.

❖ Make notes on a calendar regarding your accomplished activity. *(Example: 80 crunches, walked one mile. Made Dr. apt.)*

❖ Share your goals with at least one friend and ask them to support you.

❖ Be honest with yourself about your progress. Note the blocks to moving forward.

❖ Set a reward for yourself to be granted when the intention is met.

On The Positive Side of Life

Stay focused on the positives, the blessings, and the "GOOD" in your life. Keep a list of blessings and update it regularly – it will benefit everyone in your life, most of all you. <u>Gratitude determines attitude</u>.

Take an honest look at whether your glass is half full or half empty. If you are struggling with counting your blessings, look at lives and lifestyles in other parts of the world. Put things in perspective relative to your abundance.

Self-sympathy and blame are difficult places from which to create positive changes.

Our true character is best evaluated in times of struggle rather than times of ease. How do you handle the valleys? What is your recipe for making lemonade and finding your silver linings? Become familiar with your formula. This is where our true strength lies.

And if your cup gets empty, do not hesitate to borrow a book, purchase self-improvement CDs, go to lectures or find a good therapist.

❖ Keep a blank book in which you write down all of the positives in your life.

❖ Be aware of the people in your life that inspire and feed your creativity and those that seem to drain you of your enthusiasm.

❖ Track your "good" and "bad" days. What are the triggers for a bad day?

❖ Identify what cheers you up. Some time outdoors, perhaps? A phone call to a particular friend? A certain kind of music? Planning a little escape?

❖ Make a list of all the prideful undertakings that you have accomplished in your life, or maybe last year – or last week!

❖ Often, doing something kind for someone else can shift your "off" day. Volunteer!

❖ It may help your self-esteem to tackle some chore that has been nagging at you. Remember that our self-respect is tightly aligned with our ability to keep promises to others and ourselves.

❖ Exercise is a key mood-changer. Find a place that you enjoy going and a routine to do your chosen activity several times a week.

❖ Be aware that you are not a victim. You are in charge of shifting the thoughts, the patterns, and the mood. And a shadowed mood is easily projected onto others. *You can only give away what you have.*

Communication 101

Learn to Interview Others – Be aware of how much you talk about yourself. Attempt to shift the conversation to how the other person experienced their day, their interests, and their concerns. Learn these magical words: "Tell me more about that." Everyone is an expert on something. Ask for advice about their particular interest.

❖ **After speaking, listen for a response**. Be aware of your audience and their interest level.

❖ **Give responses that say you are engaged.** "Hmm. Really. Good."

❖ **Don't interrupt,** let them have their say.

❖ **Instead of looking around the room** – look in their eyes.

❖ **Be aware of competition** – do you pepper your conversation with a bigger and more dramatic story than the one being told to you? This is a conversation killer. Stay focused on their story. Ask for details.

❖ **Active Feedback** – it's simple. It's sweet. You repeat a little of what you are hearing in a question: "So you really enjoyed that movie?" or "How did you become interested in _____?"

❖ **Be aware of background noise/toys (music, TV, texting)** – does it eclipse what is being discussed or prevent you from being 100% engaged in the conversation?

❖ **Be careful about taking things personally and making assumptions.** These are destructive habits in a relationship.

❖ **Don't exaggerate** – you'll lose credibility. Be careful of these words: never, constantly, forever, and always.

❖ **Keep confidences**. Gossip and the delivering of information (often misinformation) is the death of intimate conversation.

❖ **Beware of imaginary agreements** – unwritten contracts that have not been discussed and agreed upon. Pat "assumed" that Chris would take responsibility for all the yard work because Pat was doing every bit of the cooking. This might be a fair exchange but the arrangement should be defined clearly - and verbally.

On Fair Fighting

First of all, let me say that conflict happens. It is part of life and hopefully it can be constructive. Here is how to keep it from getting out of hand. Please remember, when all is said and done, each of you needs to let the other know that they are loved. You have two different perspectives about an issue and the most efficient method to resolution is to let your partner have their say, and ideally, with mutual patience, they will allow you the same time to be heard.

Consider that most emotions boil down to two camps – love or fear. Arguments are usually based in Camp Fear. When a disagreement happens there has usually been an accumulation of non-discussed or unresolved issues.

And folks – this is so NOT about winning. This is about finding mutual, Happy-Camper territory. If you still think that fighting is about winning or losing, then you need to know that you have already lost. It is about mutual resolution.

We are all teachers and students to one another. Be humble enough to be a student. *Couples do not divorce because the have disagreements. They divorce because their disagreements are NOT resolved.*

Always start from this platform: Healthy conflict is about positive and constructive change within the relation-ship. Remember that you will be making up after this. The less abuse and nasty stuff the better.

Choose your battles – carefully! Ask yourself if this is really going to matter next month, next week or next year. If not, take a deep breath, close your eyes, place the misdeed into an imaginary helium balloon and release it into the atmosphere. Deep breath.

Check your mood. If you are feeling angry or resentful it will influence how you hear your partner. Try to listen and speak from a neutral place. Become familiar with your own methods of escalation and defense. Take a moment before your scheduled meeting to be in a place of accountability.

What do you really want? Can you prepare a statement requesting specific changes? Make sure that you are not just whining, that there is something particular you need from the other person.

Forgive your spouse. It is the secret to a happy married life. The sooner you master this the more blissful your life will become - guaranteed!

Forgive yourself: Be kind and gentle with yourself as well. It is difficult to take your personal inventory and shift behavior if you are pinned in by self-loathing and judgment. A miraculous occurrence follows: you will naturally become more forgiving of others!

Seldom were any of us given appropriate modeling for healthy disagreements. Healthy conflict is a learned skill that we need to practice.

Note: Whenever possible try to schedule a mutually agreeable time and topic for the requested "discussion." It is best not to react in the moment. Step back, take some time to become less emotional and mull it over. Then present the issue in a calm manner.

- ❖ No yelling. No sarcasm. No mimicking or making fun. When you or your partner are consistently speaking with an increased volume – or yelling, because of lack of control, it may be time to seek professional guidance for anger management issues.

- ❖ Name calling or cussing is forbidden.

- ❖ Threats and intimidation are not allowed. It's simply abusive. Example: "If you insist on discussing this than I'm going to bring up X, Y & Z – and you do not want to go there."

❖ Be careful of criticism. After two slams you will lose your audience.

❖ Only one person talks at a time. Nothing will be resolved if you are speaking over one another. If this rule cannot be heeded, you must get out a clock with a timer and every person gets five minutes of uninterrupted time. And these five minute turns go back and forth until you are ready to begin the resolution part of the program. And believe it or not, this often speeds up the process.

❖ Do not exaggerate – using absolute words like "always," "constantly" and "never" are nothing short of an exaggeration.

❖ Stay with the First Person, Present Tense Rule. "My feelings become hurt when you tease me about X and Y." Use "I" statements. "I feel..."

❖ A true "feeling" cannot be debated. It just is. Let it be. That is one's truth!

❖ If it gets too heated, employ the **Fight or Flight**" rule - take a break, agree to a time to resume.

❖ Own your issues – if your spouse tells you that you have been in a nasty mood ever since your best friend neglected to send you a birthday card - and you know they are right – cop to it! Tell them that it is a point well taken. Tell him/her you are really sorry – *see page 146*.

❖ You are not allowed to bring up past misdeeds, (unless the meeting is specifically intended to be on that subject matter). Stay on topic.

❖ No fighting in front of other people. That includes children. If somebody forgets this rule gently say, "Dear, remember that we agreed to have our marital meetings at home and in private?"

❖ If this argument seems to be turning into a land-fill of issues, get out a piece of paper and make a list of other issues – for other meetings, at other times. Stay on topic with the *scheduled issue*.

❖ As tempting as it is, do not even think about doing the "Tit for Tat" dance: "Well you did that too, remember?" Do listen and actively feed back their concerns in a statement form, such as, "So, you don't like when I flirt with your friend Chris and it makes you feel unloved."

❖ Do not play therapist: "Why do you think you act that way? Did your father do this to your mother?" This is a thinly veiled attack on both your partner and their family.

❖ Avoid quoting friends or relatives with personal criticisms they have made to emphasize your point. This will not foster outside relationships.

❖ If an issue has a pattern of repeating itself – it is time to get a professional involved.

The Road to Resolution:

❖ Be as respectful and as loving as possible. Try sandwiching the hurts in between a compassionate statement, like: "I know how hard you've been working lately. Yet, I need you to know that I don't feel appreciated for the extra household load I've been taking on for you. I really like to be a team player but I need to hear that you are grateful."

❖ Sprinkle your session with compassion and empathy. Try to walk a mile in their sandals.

❖ Beware of your own anger and an upsurge in negative emotion. Are you helping to provoke destructive behavior here or are you fostering creative breakthroughs?

❖ As issues are brought up, try to be accountable and respond with, "I will try harder to _____. I wasn't being sensitive to your feelings around it."

❖ This is the time you kiss and make up. Tell your sweetheart that you love them.

❖ Try to make up before bedtime. Do not let it fester and escalate. And recognize too, that at times we are better off getting a little space and cooling down.

Apologies: If you want a lasting, loving relationship, you must learn to practice this ritual. And do not think by being "kind of nice" after you misbehave is a decent substitute for a sincere and genuine apology.

Magic words for healing the situation: "I am really sorry for _____. I will try to do better next time." Please notice that there is no "but" in this statement. There is no blaming the other person for part of the issue. There is no excuse. This is *pure* accountability. Depending on the crime, you may need to ask their forgiveness. Depending on the trespass, it may take some time for it to be forgiven.

On Marriage Counseling

I advise you to find a marriage therapist specializing in couples counseling. Ideally, one you both like and would be willing to see on a regular basis in the years to come.

I recommend marriage counseling in the same way that you schedule your regular medical checkups. Yearly. It keeps things clean and healthy, balanced and nurturing.

Every couple needs to have professional support in place to help maintain a healthy relationship. A marriage is a **DYNAMIC** representing **BOTH** of the individuals. We all play off one another. The best thing any couple can do is to define how they act/react and how issues escalate. Discover what the triggers are so that peace can more easily be fostered.

Some thoughts:

❖ Find a therapist that you BOTH like. He or she should have a good sense of humor. Word of mouth is still the best way to find a reputable, caring professional.

❖ They should be licensed/certified.

❖ This therapist should make concrete suggestions that are solutions-oriented. They will hopefully recommend books that are relevant to your patterns of discord. This therapist will promote resources that support self-improvement that you can work on *in between* sessions.

❖ The marriage counselor should only used for the two of you. If either of you find that you are in need of some personal attention, hire an individual therapist for your own personal work.

❖ After a visit, you should both feel a bit lighter and never beaten up. A sense of release and awareness is the intention here. We all have issues on which to improve. Accountability is the hallmark of a marriage that is thriving.

❖ Scheduling around your wedding anniversary time will keep you on track. Consider it the greatest gift you can give each other.

Make it fun — go to dinner afterwards !

On Financial Planning

The more you are willing to discuss your future goals surrounding the way money is handled, the more you take personal responsibility for your security and ultimately the harmony of your relationship.

This issue may be one of the most volatile issues in any marriage because rarely are two individuals' spending and saving philosophies in sync. The foundation for money-based beliefs originates partly from your upbringing, your personal habits from your single days, and from our individual interests and inclinations.

Establish what monies are coming into the household and exactly how it is going out. This will take a bit of research but it will be well worth the effort. Start with the essentials: housing, utilities, insurance (medical, dental, auto), loans, etc. List the actual costs for food, transportation, clothing, and personal care. Discuss future known expenses such as household/car maintenance, medical expenses, any appliance purchases needed in the near future. Don't forget an emergency fund. Economic gurus suggest having 3-6 months worth of salary set aside – just in case.

❖ Define a realistic budget for recreation, travel and entertainment. Retirement funds need to be set in place as well. You are never too young to plan for the future.

❖ If there is credit card debt, design a strict plan to absolve it at the earliest possible time.

❖ Detail gift-giving allowances and guidelines. Christmas shopping is often lined with loving intentions, followed by dismay!

❖ A monthly allowance or a discretionary account is great idea. Personal funds to be spent or saved as your partner wishes.

❖ Another great budgeting tip: Create a mutual agreement to ask each other for permission to purchase an item over "X" dollar amount.

---

*To find a reputable financial planner ask your
friends and family whom they trust.*

If a baby is in your future, this needs to be discussed as a financial consideration as well. In addition to the medical cost, childcare has become financially prohibitive. More mothers and fathers are choosing to be "stay at home" parents because of this. Research the expense of raising a child (there are tables on the Internet). The cost range at this writing (depending on your income and educational preferences), is between $350,000 - $1,000,000. This is for 6,500 days. And then there is college! Again, it is never too soon to plan for the future.

Update your financial plan once a year. Jobs change, the economic climate is always in flux and personal priorities, interests and goals are reordered.

YOUR BALANCED MISSION STATEMENT

By creating this statement of intentions together, you will both have input into the strategy that best suits the type of marriage that you choose to build.

Your Mission Statement will change because both of you will change. This is an exercise that would behoove you to update at least once a year. This is a short exercise that is a constructive investment in the well-being of your future relationship.

And it is easier than you realize. In this chapter you will find a sample Mission Statement template with fill-in-the-blanks (on page 153). Go to the appropriate selection of words designated for the particular paragraph to decide what will best suit your relationship (pages 155, 156). This process will help clarify the undefined.

To get started, agree with your sweetheart on a date and time for a meeting and find a quiet and positive environment with no distractions.

There are five basic topics in writing this mission statement that profoundly relates to your marriage partnership. You may decide to add additional writings. Be creative and feel free to use your own words to fill in the blanks.

The Theme of Your Foundation

You will find a "fill-in-the blanks" Mission Statement in this chapter on page 153. For the first paragraph of your Mission Statement, choose as many words as you like. The Foundation Paragraph is essential in providing insights in defining your relationship. And this will be a work in progress. Be aware of it, discuss it, and edit it. When talking with your loved one, keep in mind that this paragraph will anchor the life you establish together. So, you'll want to select words that are true for you. *Please see "Suggested Word List for Balanced Mission Statement" on page 155.*

Couple Renewal

What is your plan for couple rejuvenation? Remember, keeping it fresh might become more challenging as time goes on. And all of creation needs to be recharged from time to time. Your relationship is no different. The intention here is to consistently increase intimacy by including experiences you will plan to do together. Be specific with time – some revitalization needs to take place daily, some weekly or monthly. Plan two or more getaways per year, without friends, family or children! And be detailed with each plan, specifically stating each goal. You might begin by brainstorming the methods that most rekindle your spirits – then discuss the frequency and budgets for these escapes. *Please see "Suggested Word List for Balanced Mission Statement" on page 155.*

Finely Tuned Communication

The third paragraph will tackle the cornerstone of communication. There are lots of books on the subject. Check out the suggested reading list in the chapter. Be sure you can play by the rules of what the author is suggesting, because you will be expected to live by the creed you select. Buy it, keep it handy. This will be your sanity during times of disagreement and negotiation. The blank in paragraph three is for the name of your chosen book and/or author/lecturer. Feel free to list the enclosed "Quick Guide" as a short term or long term resource. *Please see "Suggested Word List for Balanced Mission Statement" on page 156.*

Maintenance of the Marriage

Paragraph No. 4 will help sustain your marriage. Define how you are going to keep it fine-tuned. What professional are you going to trust to guide you along the journey? What tools will you use?

Suggestion: Couples ideally find a mutually acceptable marriage therapist and make an appointment each year around their anniversary time. This needs to happen whether they think that they "need to" or not. Recently, after 15 years of marriage, a client wrote to me and said this was the best advice I had given to them. Two children, a new home business and a Master's degree later and they are still thriving. *Please see "Suggested Word List for Balanced Mission Statement" on page 156.*

Positive Development

Mutual support is needed when maintaining individual balance. This part of your mission statement may change. Marriage is a tight interaction of two people. If either becomes destabilized, there will be an upset in the equilibrium of the partnership. *Please see "Suggested Word List for Balanced Mission Statement" on page 156.*

Here is the "fill in the blanks" template of your mission statement. Feel free to embellish with additional phrases and words to fit your individual plan.

_____ and _____'s Balanced Mission Statement

Date: _____

Paragraph #1, Foundation

As a married couple _____ and _____ recognize their marriage is based on_____. We choose it to be our foundation, upon which all other elements of marriage are built.

Paragraph #2, Couple Renewal

We are both committed to upholding our vows and realize that marriage is the act of choosing to be in love and we will consciously work towards renewal and romance specifically through _____, _____ and, _____.

Paragraph #3, Communication Skills

Understanding that communication is an essential element to the balance of the marital atmosphere, we mutually subscribe to creating a peaceful life together by practicing the principals found in _____. (Specific name of book, with author or seminar.)

Paragraph #4, Maintenance

We further realize our dedication, support, and love will only increase through continued maintenance. Our chosen methods to grow our balanced marriage will be through _____, _____ and _____.

Paragraph # 5, Individual Balance

Understanding that each of us are individuals and have specific needs, there will be a respected and mutual agreement of support for individual creativity, health and balance. _____ will lovingly encourage _____ to continue to schedule and pursue activities in _____,_____ and _____. In turn, _____ will support _____'s interests and involvement in _____, _____, and _____.

(Please note: financial goals may be addressed in an additional paragraph.)

Suggested Word List for Balanced Mission Statement

Paragraph One: Foundation

Trust

Love

Loyalty

God

Compassion

Friendship

Honesty

Commitment

Faith

Unity

Equality

Paragraph Two: Couple Renewal

Laughter

Playing Together

Weekly dates

Lessons (Dance, Cooking, Language)

Daily verbal communication of appreciation

Travel/Get-aways (couple being alone)

Romance (describe)

Prayer

Meditation

Study Groups

Retreats

Paragraph Three: Communication Skills

Book/Author
Seminar/Lecturer
Rev. Mary's Quick Guide

Paragraph Four: Maintenance

Compromise
Respect
Accountability
Autonomy
Time to play
Exercise
Counseling for the couple (at least once a year is ideal)
Volunteering in the community

Paragraph Five: Individual Balance

Exercise/sports
Journaling
Individual
Counseling
Medical/ dental checkups, medication
Massage
Healthy eating habits, vitamins
Getting away with old friends
Seeing their family of origin
Meditation
Reading – books of self-help and inspiration
Seeking a spiritual life

Taking classes
Pursuing new hobbies or learning new skills
Yoga
Study groups
Bubble Baths
Sauna/Hot tub/Spa days
Beauty Treatments/Facials

"Happily Ever After" Suggested Reading List:

Conscience Loving by Gay Hendricks and Kathlyn Hendricks

The Ten Laws of Lasting Love by Paul Pearsall

Intimate Partners by Maggie Scarf

Expansive Marriage by J. Donald Walters

Seven Secrets of a Happy Marriage by Margery D. Rosen

The 5 Love Languages by Gary D. Chapman

The 5 Love Languages: The Secret to Love That Lasts by Gary D. Chapman

The Seven Principles for Making Marriage Work by John M. Gottman, PH.D. and Nan Silver

What Makes Love Last? by John M. Gottman, PH.D. and Nan Silver

Lies at the Altar – The Truth About Great Marriages by Dr. Robin L. Smith

Love and Respect by Dr. Emerson Eggerichs

As Long as We Both Shall Live by Dr. Gary Smalley and Ted Cunningham

Made in the USA
Lexington, KY
06 September 2016